METAPHORS
FOR THE
CONTEMPORARY
CHURCH

METAPHORS FOR THE CONTEMPORARY CHURCH

Susan Brooks Thistlethwaite

THE PILGRIM PRESS
New York

Scripture quotations, unless otherwise indicated, are from the
Revised Standard Version of the Bible, copyright 1946, 1952 and
© 1971, 1973 by the Division of Christian Education, National
Council of Churches, and are used by permission. The scripture
quotation marked KJV is from the *King James Version.* Scripture
quotations marked NEB are from *The New English Bible.* © The
Delegates of the Oxford University Press and The Syndics of the
Cambridge University Press, 1961, 1970. Reprinted by permission.

Library of Congress Cataloging in Publication Data

Thistlethwaite, Susan Brooks, 1948–
  Metaphors for the contemporary church.

  Includes bibliographical references.
  1. Church. I. Title.
BV600.2.T486   1983   262   83-13438
ISBN 0-8298-0692-X (pbk.)

The Pilgrim Press, 132 West 31 Street, New York, NY 10001

This book is dedicated to my husband,
J. Richard Thistlethwaite Jr.,
and our two sons,
James and William,
with a prayer for our continued closeness

Contents

Foreword

THIS IS a pioneer work. Susan Thistlethwaite writes with great commitment to the church. Feminist thinkers have taken many tacks in order to alter our North American perception of gender roles; this book is adamant on not giving up on the church as feminist consciousness is growing.

The wide-ranging argument will evoke many responses of the imagination. From Junia to Elisabeth Schüssler Fiorenza; from Tertullian to Gutiérrez; from primitive church to ecumenical movement—one is constantly alerted to a variety of voices which yet form a unified theme.

What brings us close to the center of the argument is the invitation to a new self-awareness of the church: "The flat and nearly antiecclesiological language of American Protestantism both reflects and permits the cultural accommodation so typical of American Protestantism. Yet . . . metaphors for the church can draw the church out toward renewed self-awareness."

This book provokes us to examine our prejudgments on many points. We have to re-think and re-tool. The reflections on the body of Christ are among the most crucial. The church has often forgotten the importance of "body." Women and "the poor"—to use Thistlethwaite's metaphor—are less likely to forget it. Whenever the church tends either to become rigid as institution or co-opted by the culture, it needs to be reminded that it is the body of Christ, in the world, but not of the world, embodying God's spirit without controlling it.

Women and "the poor" know the value of bodiliness, of vulnerability, cooperation, receptiveness, nurture, and compassion. What Susan Thistlethwaite, quoting Schleiermacher, calls the "bodily side of the matter," or, in her own words, the "messy, conflictual, and many-faceted historical reality"—this is what women and "the poor" can point to in a society that prefers easy harmony among splintered denominations and smooth efficiency through traditional patriarchal structures.

Democracy is a tedious, tension-filled process as compared with patriarchal kingship, and yet the United States opted for it long ago. Equal justice for women and other second-class groups is a continuation of the struggle for democracy. Likewise, the Reformation's emphasis on the equality of all believers continues in the expression of a woman's right to ordination and leadership roles in the church.

Feminists have come a long way from telling women to break into male professions and do what men do, just as blacks in this country have come a long way from simply trying to do what whites have been able to do all along. We have recognized that our "bodies"—our gender or race heritage and even our geographic locations—are all important parts of the body politic as well as the body of Christ; that their uniqueness has to be cherished; and that tensions among them can be creative instead of destructive—if justice prevails over privilege.

The medieval Great Chain of Being was turned upside down in the nineteenth century. Romanticism valued the bottom of the ladder of Being. In our time, we need to forget about "top" or "bottom" and forge a chain of justice which allows each human body to stand and move on the same ground, with the same intensity. If the church can form a chain of justice as concrete and as vulnerable as the chain of human bodies British women were able to build for peace in 1982, it will be on its way to be truly the body of Christ. Susan Thistlethwaite is a "welder" for such a chain.

This is not a book simply to "agree with." The author's integrity of conviction, clarity of purpose, and awareness of need is a strong contagion going far beyond agreement or disagreement on particular points. It is a work that inspires us to continue welding the links in the Great Chain of Justice. How can the church be part of this chain? How can the church be inclusive without losing its identity as the body of Christ? How can the church witness to the authority of Christ without becoming authoritarian? Even if you do not find your answer in this book, you certainly will be inspired to creative thinking of your own. You no longer will be the same. It is that kind of germinative book.

Kristin and Frederick Herzog
Durham, North Carolina

Preface

WHILE NOT a manifesto, this book is written out of a sense of urgency. Women and men are trained by seminary faculty who are becoming sensitized to the issues raised by the women's movement, without being given the opportunity to explore what this changed perspective means for the church they are called to serve. This is particularly poignant for women, who have good reason to regard the church as the enemy. This view is frequently reinforced by experiences with church structures that block access to decision-making processes.

Women and men in the church are caught by a sense of frustration as declining memberships and salvos from the far right call into question the traditional values of the mainline Protestant Church. Both laypeople and clergy are threatened by individual constituencies such as women, blacks, Chicanos, and the poor, all of whom are demanding a say in the structures of the church. Such demands seem only further to divide and weaken the church.

It seems we have passed the point in feminist theology where "ain't it awful" suffices. The point is not to complain about the church, but to change it (to paraphrase Marx). This book, therefore, is not an attempt to help women relate better to the church as it is, but to argue for a more authentic approach to the doctrine of the church for all Christians. It will be argued that when any group is systematically excluded from the community of the church, the church can fail to be the church. But an inclusive church is a possibility for renewed strength and power for social change, a strength that comes from cooperation and a power that comes from sharing. These times cry out for such a church.

I am deeply appreciative of all the religious communities to which I have belonged for the sense of the possibilities for human bonding they gave me: Wesley Theological Seminary, Chicago Theological Seminary, the Women's Theological Center, and especially Eliot United Church of Christ, Newton, Massachusetts.

Many individuals also helped. The Rev. Sandra Hughes Boyd, reference librarian at the Episcopal Divinity School in Cambridge, Massachusetts, was especially generous with her time. My dear friend Robin Darling read several drafts and gave me invaluable comments with her intense scholarship and unremitting honesty. I should also like to thank Herb Davis, pastor of Eliot Church; John Westerhoff; Carter Heyward; and, of course, Fred and Kristin Herzog. With Fred and Kristin I have shared a vision of what the church can be through the caring and social witness of Pilgrim United Church of Christ, Durham, North Carolina.

Students at the seminaries at which I have worked deserve my special thanks for never accepting anything I said in classes without questioning and probing. I wrote this book for them.

**METAPHORS
FOR THE
CONTEMPORARY
CHURCH**

The Welder

I AM A WELDER.
NOT AN ALCHEMIST.
I AM INTERESTED IN THE BLEND
OF COMMON ELEMENTS TO MAKE
A COMMON THING.

NO MAGIC HERE.
ONLY THE HEAT OF MY DESIRE TO FUSE
WHAT I ALREADY KNOW
EXISTS. IS POSSIBLE.

WE PLEAD TO EACH OTHER,
WE ALL COME FROM THE SAME ROCK
WE ALL COME FROM THE SAME ROCK
IGNORING THE FACT THAT WE BEND
AT DIFFERENT TEMPERATURES
THAT EACH OF US IS MALLEABLE
UP TO A POINT.

YES, FUSION IS POSSIBLE
BUT ONLY IF THINGS GET HOT ENOUGH—
ALL ELSE IS TEMPORARY ADHESION,
PATCHING UP.

IT IS THE INTIMACY OF STEEL MELTING
INTO STEEL, THE FIRE OF OUR INDIVIDUAL
PASSION TO TAKE HOLD OF OURSELVES
THAT MAKES SCULPTURE OF OUR LIVES,
BUILDS BUILDINGS.

AND I AM NOT TALKING ABOUT SKYSCRAPERS,
MERELY STRUCTURES THAT CAN SUPPORT US
WITHOUT FEAR
OF TREMBLING.

FOR TOO LONG A TIME
THE HEAT OF MY HEAVY HANDS
HAS BEEN SMOLDERING
IN THE POCKETS OF OTHER
PEOPLE'S BUSINESS—
THEY NEED OXYGEN TO MAKE FIRE.

I AM NOW
COMING UP FOR AIR.
YES, I AM
PICKING UP THE TORCH.

I AM THE WELDER.
I UNDERSTAND THE CAPACITY OF HEAT
TO CHANGE THE SHAPE OF THINGS.
I AM SUITED TO WORK
WITHIN THE REALM OF SPARKS
OUT OF CONTROL.

I AM THE WELDER.
I AM TAKING THE POWER
INTO MY OWN HANDS.

—Cherríe Moraga*

*From *This Bridge Called My Back*, 2d ed., 1983. Kitchen Table/Women of Color Press, Rockefeller Center Station, New York, NY 10185. Used by permission.

Method

METHOD IS the constructional system which gives theology its infrastructure and strength. Feminist theological method must have unusual tensile strength and flexibility to stand firmly on the shifting ground of contemporary struggles for liberation.

Method should contain a statement of why a project has been undertaken. A clear statement of the purpose of a project not only gives it shape but direction.

WHY THE CHURCH?

AS I have been working on this book, many people have asked, "Why the church?" That is the last topic they expect a feminist to be researching. But the "why" of this book follows quite naturally from the beginning point of feminist theology. Feminist theologians tend to begin with their experience. Because women's experience has so often been denied to be universally human, the beginning point for almost all feminist thought is a recovery of the specifics of women's experience. But this is not experience conceived only as reflection on the subjective self, but includes experience of objective forces within history. Women's experience *of* the church as it shapes their historical reality is one "why" for this project.

Women who have studied the church have focused almost exclusively on women's experience with its actual, institutional makeup, especially as its functioning has excluded women. Mary Daly's *The Church and the Second Sex* (1972) and the collection edited by Alice Hageman, *Sexist Religion and Women in the Church: "No More Silence!"* (1974), "grope for words to express experienced realities which men in power are too often glad to deny."[1] Theology, and especially ecclesiology (the doctrine of the church), has not traditionally begun with the existential church. Instead, theologians have focused on a theoretical formulation about the church—that it is, for example, the repository of the one true faith—and have developed their statements about the actual, existential church in light of this formulation.

One major component of the method used in this work is a challenge to that traditional standpoint. This study will begin with the actual, existential church and analyze power relationships in that institution as these have had an impact on theological reflection.

WHY WOMEN'S EXPERIENCE?

WOMEN'S experience has been chosen because it provides insight into these power relationships from the perspective of some of those who have been denied power in the institution. Doing ecclesiology from an analysis of relationships within the institution of the church means that sources other than traditional theology must be found in order to develop the critical tools for such analysis. Women are beginning to analyze the sources of their exclusion. One such study is Jean Baker Miller's powerful book *Toward a New Psychology of Women.*

Miller makes the point that societies emphasize some qualities for dominant groups and other qualities for subordinates. In male-led societies, women have been associated with the caretaker functions of home maintenance and child rearing and hence have been assigned those behaviors that best enable them to care for others. These are cooperation, integration, and affiliation, as well as vulnerability, weakness, helplessness, and dependency.[2]

The reason societies do this is to "manage" certain traits for survival purposes, emphasizing external aggression against competitors for food, while at the same time managing to relate internally as a society. Miller observes:

> Another important aspect of women's psychology is their greater recognition of the essential cooperative nature of human existence. Despite the competitive aspects of any society, there must be a bedrock modicum of cooperativeness for society to exist at all. (I define cooperative as behavior that aids and enhances the development of other human beings while advancing one's own.) It is certainly clear that we have not reached a very high level of cooperative living. To the extent that it exists, women have assumed the greater responsibility for providing it.[3]

While initially this division of human traits may have had some useful survival function, in an increasingly global village survival may depend on integrating the values projected solely onto women into the whole human psyche.

Miller's thesis provides the social and psychological framework in which to discern not only that the values of cooperation, integration, and affiliation are assigned to women in Western cultures, but also to discern *for the first time* that these are also the values that the biblical materials advance as representing God's will for the whole human community. Some obvious examples of this are the servant images of Isaiah with which Jesus repeatedly identified himself and which he stressed for the community of the disciples, and Paul's admonition to the Corinthians in 1 Corinthians 13 that communal relations in Christ are animated by love.

Paradoxically, the church has frequently denigrated these same values of cooperation, integration, and affiliation and often has reflected the larger society in relegating them to women.

Utilizing the framework developed by Miller, it is possible to examine the church with particularly close attention to the issue of values. It seems plausible that an examination of the inclusion or exclusion of women in any given period of the church's history would indicate the prevailing values of the church. If, as Miller observes, women represent certain values, when these are in operation, women will tend to be well represented. When other, contradictory values are functioning, women will be excluded.

Furthermore, if these values of cooperation, integration, and affiliation do represent faithfully the will of God for human community, then it may be possible to gauge the faithfulness of the church's behavior to the biblical witness by examining the dominant values. And it may be possible to reinterpret ecclesiology so that the church may be more consistently called to incarnate these values.

WHY METAPHOR?

IT is extremely difficult to get at the question of the dominant values operative in any given period of the life of the church. One possible way is to focus on the prevailing metaphors or images in use for the church at the time. Paul Minear, in his exhaustive study *Images of the Church in the New Testament*, says that images are

> a mode for perceiving a given reality, especially when this reality is of such a nature as not to be amenable to objective study or measurement. Any reality that is inherently a mystery will demand for its perception an awakening of the imagination.[4]

Images are a description of the church that reflects its self-understanding and also creates self-understanding, but in ways that defy objective description.

A metaphor is a type of image even less descriptive of the perceived object. There is even much debate over what, in fact, constitutes a metaphor and how it is supposed to function.[5] Frederick Herzog has noted that the function of biblical metaphors is to break imaginative boundaries.

> What the Gospel as praxis text of theology brings out is the predominantly metaphorical character of Gospel language. It does not transfer meaning to

a deeper or higher reality, nor does it primarily conceptualize reality. It creates new reality. In the light of the newly created reality, reality as a whole is questioned, acted upon and interpreted in a new way.[6]

Metaphor expresses the heuristic power of thought, which moves from the known to the unknown and enables new knowledge to emerge by association. When we investigate the unknown we ask, "What is it like?" Our answer in metaphor conveys both a likeness and an unlikeness. Metaphor creates new reality by introducing a tension of both likeness and unlikeness, which enables the reality of our experience to be reexamined. Metaphor is the way thought moves; it is thought in action.[7] When metaphors lose this tension, there is a loss of power. In speaking at the level of image, a less intense type of metaphor, Minear describes this loss. The church's

> self-understanding, its inner cohesion, its *esprit de corps* derive from a dominant image of itself. . . . If an unauthentic image dominates its consciousness, there will first be subtle signs of malaise, followed by more overt tokens of communal deterioration. If an authentic image is recognized at the verbal level, but denied in practice, there will also follow sure disintegration of the ligaments of corporate life.[8]

There are few who would deny that the church suffers from just such a malaise today. The church in a post-Christendom world has to work doubly hard to achieve a sense of itself—it is no longer a given of the modern world view. The modern world, in fact, appears to work very hard to stamp upon the church a prevailing image drawn from culture, as patron saint of the nation-state.

The question that must be addressed is how the church can recover a sense of itself appropriate both to the current cultural climate and to the church's ongoing life. These are not separate issues, but must be treated in tandem. Both the world and the church are changing constantly. There is continuity, certainly, but there is also discontinuity and a consequent need for change. Thus, some metaphors may now better speak to the church's self than others.

Paul Minear lists ninety-six images for the church in his study of the New Testament. This proliferation, evident in only one short slice of the church's history, precludes exhaustive research into each way the church has imaged itself for historical patterns or organization and contemporary applications. Some selective principle must be brought to bear.

Inclusivity versus exclusivity regarding women is the approach selected here. Because women can be shown to have represented certain values in the history of at least Western society, their representation is a bellwether for other out-groups of society. Furthermore, the signs of the times have shown that the inclusion of women in the mainstream of church and society is a crisis in modern Western consciousness. But it is necessary that the criterion of inclusivity versus exclusivity regarding women not be applied apart from a historical context. The intimate relationship between metaphor and experience means that only in community can a given metaphor be understood.

It is striking to note how many times the words image or metaphor appear in the dissertation titles of women listed in the *Registry of Women in Religious Studies*. The frequent use of these words suggests a different way of thinking about religious studies on the part of women scholars.

Academic study in religion since the Renaissance has emphasized the conceptual pole of thought in which the key to understanding religious phenomena is found in dissection and examination of each contributing component. But women's studies have often emphasized imagistic, metaphorical modes of thought. They challenge the notion that theological understanding comes solely from objective, rationalistic analysis divorced from synthetic, imaginative thought. Women have learned through consciousness-raising efforts that the truest understanding often comes not from division, but from integration of otherwise seemingly disconnected ideas in order to imagine new possibilities. The use of metaphor as a methodological tool for getting to the church's awareness of itself, and for *changing* this awareness, comes out of my conviction that theological discourse today needs to recognize the continuum between image and concept, and to take more account of the imagistic basis of all thought.[9]

WHY THE THEOLOGY OF LIBERATION?

ANOTHER essential element in theological method from a feminist perspective, along with the personal and the social, is the political. It is a maxim of women's groups that the personal *is* the political: individual problems created by sexism are part of a larger system of oppression and cannot be treated in isolation.

Here the important contribution of the theologians of liberation in Latin America to the development of a theological method is to insist that the theological task involves political and economic analysis. The tools for this critical task come primarily, but not exclusively, from Marxist views of history, which help reveal the economic forces at work in creating and sustaining theological doctrine. Christians need to face up to the ecclesiological task for a church enmeshed in the patterns of domination and oppression of the powerless. Without clarity about this involvement and the means to evaluate it critically, the doctrine of the church may remain part of the reigning social ideology and be unable to attain the distance necessary to criticize injustice in the larger society.[10]

The assumption of a critical role for psychological, social, political, and economic analysis in the theological task is a new vantage point for theology. The theological task is no longer conceived exclusively as a rationalistic, deductive task of prescription, but rather is, as Gustavo Gutiérrez has said, the second act. Theology is impossible without the first act, which is the living out of the faith in relationship to God active in history. Theologians are called upon to become involved with and to critically reflect on the working out of our historical task as Christians.

WHY THEOLOGY AND ETHICS?

PUSHING still farther into this process, which has been called the "hermeneutical circle," we Christians must come clean and admit our responsibility for the ethical consequences of our theological statements. That is to say, we must hold on and come full circle, to a recognition that the second act of theology leads to a third act, which is a response to our reflections.

Let us for clarity's sake take two examples. If we

elaborate a type of just-war doctrine in reflection on the faithful struggle of Christians in violently repressive situations, we are responsible for continuing to hold our theological eyes and ears open as we participate in what Dom Helder Camara has called the spiral of violence and to recognize that we must live and reflect again on the consequences of what we have said.

Or, if we are willing to separate our life into a doctrine of two kingdoms, we are not free from responsibility when the two kingdoms divide our life as Christians and paralyze social action. The ethical consequences of theological doctrines must become part of a critical reevaluation of those doctrines. Theology as the second act participates as well in the actions that follow reflection.

FROM WHY TO HOW

THE theological method proposed, therefore, is one that takes the particularity of the contemporary Christian situation seriously and holds that it is impossible to function theologically unless we move through this particularity toward more general categories. This particularity is a prime datum for theological reflection, to which are brought the tools of psychological, social, political, and economic analysis in a creative tension with the more traditional sources for theology— biblical witness, church tradition, philosophy, and the like. But this entire critical apparatus is understood as reflecting on and in turn contributing to the faithful action of the people of God in history. The whole process is best understood from a primarily associational mode of thought such as metaphor represents.

Therefore, chapter 1 examines metaphors that have

been used by Christians to understand their experience of the church in three periods of the church's life: the earliest church, the medieval period, and nineteenth-century Protestantism. While many other historical periods could also have formed part of this examination, these three have been chosen because they illustrate issues crucial in the contemporary Protestant Church. This section does not pretend to be an in-depth historical analysis, but a sketch of some tendencies that have had an impact on the contemporary church.

Some metaphors chosen speak to a more inclusive self-understanding and are tied to the recognition of inclusivity, especially with regard to women, as a value for the church. Others speak to an exclusive self-understanding, and the exclusion of women appears to be part of this view. The sum of an investigation into inclusive and exclusive metaphors yields the insight that the Miller thesis appears to obtain for church organization. When the church allows women to be prominent, it appears to value cooperative, integrative, and egalitarian structures. When women are excluded from prominence in the church, structure tends to be pyramidal, hierarchical, and authoritarian.

Chapter 2 makes a transition between these historical observations and the contemporary situation of the church. Experience-based theology demands a contextualization of theological discourse, and the difference between the contexts of North America and South America is now a crucial issue in theology. This chapter addresses the question of which metaphors speak best to the experience of the South American Church and which speak to the North American. The argument is made that the North American Church needs to be confronted by the metaphors of the Body of Christ and the Poor as those metaphors address the particular social and economic problems of the church in North America.

Chapter 3 examines Christology in terms of the metaphor of the Body of Christ. Christologies that have led the church to division and stratification will not enable this metaphor to shape experience. Christologies that have excluded women call out a self-understanding of the church which is predominantly hierarchical and authoritarian and hence do not actualize this metaphor. Inclusive Christologies speak to a self-understanding that is cooperative, integrative, and egalitarian and enable Christians to be truly the Body in practice.

Chapter 4 continues the theological restructuring by examining in depth the metaphor of the Poor, with an emphasis on the Holy Spirit as the spirit of justice in human relationships. While we Christians attempt to incarnate ourselves as the Body of Christ, we must also deal with political aspects of being the church in the world. North American white suburban Protestants, the largest constituency of this book, are not the poor. The situation of the North American Protestant Church demands that it struggle to experience the presence of the Holy Spirit as the spirit of justice, to challenge it in its affluence, and to enable it to stand alongside the poor in their struggles for social and economic justice.

Chapter 5 applies this renewed theological base to an agenda for the North American Church. The women's movement is an example of the type of church structure that is rooted in the values of cooperation, integration, and affiliation and that actualizes the metaphor of the Body of Christ. While cognizant of its problems, the women's movement points to ways in which the church can be both pluralistic in its constituencies and universal in its intent. As Protestant and Catholic white women struggle to be in the church in deed, they also struggle with their own racism. Addressing race and class among themselves, women in the movement demonstrate that the personal is the political and that their separation is a false dualism. Furthermore, their struggle indicates that the rise of a political consciousness of the need for solidarity with the poor is the key to the renewal of the church in North America.

This fact makes the growing nuclear freeze movement in the churches in North America another example of a church that takes its political responsibility seriously. The nuclear freeze campaign as a grass-roots movement in the churches has avoided many of the errors of the antiwar movement, such as denominational insularity and elitism. The antinuclear forces are working within local churches to bring about a public protest to continued arms buildup and to the cuts in social programs that threaten the lives of the poor. Women such as Helen Caldicott, founder of Physicians for Social Responsibility, have been very prominent in this movement.

These two examples demonstrate the already existent places where the metaphors of the Body of Christ and the Poor can speak to the privatized, divided character of the North American Protestant denominational church.

The concluding chapter is a meditation on the relationships between authority, power, and hierarchy. The question addressed in this final section is whether authority necessitates hierarchy. The sources of the authority of an inclusive church that is public and political are examined.

Chapter 1 WOMEN AND METAPHOR IN THE HISTORY OF THE CHURCH

METAPHOR IS thought in action. Metaphor reveals the deepest experiences of human beings and impels them to act in new ways. Metaphor has frequently been employed by Christians in the history of the church both to describe their communal experience and to motivate themselves to repentance and change.

An examination of three periods in the life of the church reveals two distinct types of metaphor: inclusive and exclusive. In this work, inclusive and exclusive refer to the inclusion or exclusion of women in the power structures of the church. It is also possible to generalize from women to other groups traditionally considered second-class humans, such as persons of color and the poor.

Metaphors that reflect inclusivity with regard to women are also reflective of an open, egalitarian approach to church structure. Alternatively, metaphors that speak to an exclusive understanding of the church with regard to women reflect an insistence on closed, hierarchical systems.

THE EARLY CHURCH

The New Creation

Jesus, as the Gospels portray him, initiated a movement that was inclusive and egalitarian in style. He excluded no one from his circle who wished to follow him: prostitutes, tax collectors, lepers, outcasts of all kinds. Even the hated Roman military was invited in. Whenever the disciples attempted to exclude someone, Jesus rebuked them (Mark 9:38-40; 10:13-16).[1]

It is this novelty, this genuinely new thing that was happening in history to which the metaphor New Creation speaks. "When anyone is united to Christ, there is a new act of creation; the old order has gone, and a new order has already begun [2 Cor. 5:17, NEB]." The newness of the way Jesus' followers were instructed to relate to one another reflected the act of God in Christ, a new creation. This novelty contrasted sharply with the old way of doing things: the old order slavishly subject, fearful of its own liberation.[2]

A large part of this novelty was Jesus' astonishing openness to the full participation of women among his followers. Followers of Jesus are disciples, those who hear the Word and do it (Mark 8:34-35). By this definition, the Synoptics agree that women were among the most faithful of Jesus' disciples. Women were at the foot of the cross, remaining when many of the other disciples had fled (Matthew 27:55; Mark

15:47; Luke 23:49). They were the ones who found the tomb empty (Matthew 28:1-6; Mark 16:1-5; Luke 24:3); the announcement of Jesus' resurrection is first made to women (Matthew 28:5-7; Mark 16:6; Luke 24:5-7); Jesus appeared first to women and commissioned them to tell of his resurrection, the central fact of the "good news," to the other disciples (Matthew 28:10; Mark 16:7; Luke 24:8-9).

The Roman Catholic Church has emphasized the absence of women among the twelve disciples as evidence of Jesus' preference for male leadership.[3] While the New Testament authors are not uniformly in agreement on the role of the twelve, the theological function of the twelve is to represent the twelve tribes of Israel. In this way they provide a bridge between the Israelite past and the hoped-for future in which all Jews and Gentiles would be united as the People of God.[4] The function of the twelve is not related to any set leadership role, since with the exceptions of Peter, James, and John (see Galatians 2:9), they are not seen in this character in the church. Consistent with their largely symbolic and not administrative role, they were not replaced by the church after their deaths.

Much of the New Testament material leads one to believe that the circle around Jesus was in fact quite fluid and did include women. Another title for Jesus' followers throughout his ministry is apostles. Generally, the term apostle is thought to refer to the twelve, a point of view held by the framers of the Vatican Declaration. On the contrary, it is a much wider circle, according to some New Testament writers.[5] Junia, considered a woman by John Chrysostom, is named by Paul as "outstanding among the Apostles." (The apostle Paul was, of course, not a member of the twelve; see Galatians 1:11ff.)

It is, therefore, reasonable to conclude that women were included among the most intimate circle of Jesus' followers, and that this openness was a deliberate choice on Jesus' part, a practice in direct contrast to that of the patriarchal culture in which he lived.

But not only was the circle around Jesus open in terms of membership, it was open in terms of decision-making style. When James and John evidenced a desire to trade on their closeness to him and throw their weight about, Jesus countered with a lecture on what his followers' pattern of relationship should be.

> You know that in the world the recognized rulers lord it over their subjects, and their great men make them feel the weight of authority. That is not the way with you; among you, whoever wants to be great must be your servant, and whoever wants to be first must be the willing slave of all.
> —Mark 10:42-44, NEB

See also Mark 12:38-40; Luke 11:43.

This point also affirms that an exclusive group, the twelve, is unlikely to have been Jesus' choice for a closed ministry like the hereditary Levitical priesthood. On the contrary, this is precisely the sort of exclusivity Jesus decried (Luke 12:1-3).

The evangelists were clear that the pattern Jesus laid down was to be valid for the church. Within the earliest church, status jobs were abolished; the church was not to use the honorific titles rabbi, father, master (Matthew 23:8-10). There were no religious specialists: "A disciple is not above his teacher, but every one when he is fully taught will be like his teacher [Luke 6:40]." Robin Scroggs has asserted: "Outside of the Church of Jerusalem, there do not seem to have been any hierarchical structures in the beginning; deacons, elders and bishops appear only later."[6]

Women were not excluded from full participation in this open system. Despite androcentric interpretation and redaction, it can be shown, as Elisabeth Schüssler Fiorenza has done time and again, that in the early church "women were missionaries, apostles or heads of communities."[7]

The metaphor of the New Creation applies to the experience of the newness of life in the earliest Christian communities. The full participation of women in these communities is an essential part of this changed human condition.

The Body of Christ

Another metaphor used for the church in the New Testament period is the Body of Christ. In this metaphor, the relationship of community members to one another is described in organic, wholistic terms.

In 1 Corinthians 12, Paul explicitly describes the church as the body of Christ; the point of the metaphor is the abolition of hierarchical distinctions between the church members: "For Christ is like a single body with its many limbs and organs, which, many as they are, together make up one body. . . . Now you are Christ's body, and each of you a limb or organ of it [1 Cor. 12:12, 27, NEB]."

The problem the Corinthian church faced was an oversupply of spiritual gifts, the exercise of which was fostering competition and dissension among the members, especially during worship. All spiritual gifts come from God, wrote Paul, and are meant to serve God's ends, the common good. The Body metaphor was used by Paul to convey the ideal of a communal structure in which all have different functions, but in which all play an equally important role.

When a person joined this community, the rite of passage, baptism, reflected a unity of equals. Galatians 3:28 is now widely regarded as a fragment of an early baptismal formula:[8] "Baptized into union with him, you have all put on Christ as a garment. There is no such thing as Jew and Greek, slave and free . . . , male and female; for you are all one person in Christ Jesus [Gal. 3:27-28, NEB]."

Paul's letters indicate that many women exercised the charismata of leadership and that their authority for so doing rested precisely on this view that there are many varieties of gifts, but only one Spirit. In 1 Corinthians 11:5-16, Paul acknowledges a woman's right to prophesy in the community, though he also bows to patriarchal tradition and requires that a woman do so with a covered head.

At the same time it is emphasized that Paul clearly felt he could not deny the gift of prophecy when a woman was given it by the Spirit of God. In Acts 2:17-21, Peter declares, quoting Joel, that the Spirit is poured out on both sons and daughters.[9]

Paul used the metaphor of the church as the Body of Christ not in order to recognize a unity that already existed, but to stimulate the imagination of the Corinthians so that they might strive to create among themselves the kind of cooperation, integration, and affiliation that would make them truly one. 1 Corinthians 13 follows logically upon this schema, because the "more excellent way" is the way of love. The gift of love is the primary means of building up the interdependence of the church's members. This is the gift that makes all the others possible. The metaphor of the church as the Body of Christ is, therefore, incomplete without that of love. 1 Corinthians 13 is not primarily a homily to the individual on the virtues of being nice, but a major ecclesiastical statement on the way in which the members of the church become the Body of Christ. The way of love that binds the Body together is a way in which the gifts of all, including women, add to the whole and none is deemed more valuable than all.

Headship

In the pseudo-Pauline epistles a shift in emphasis occurs. In Colossians, for example, the Headship of Christ is the predominant metaphor for the church (Colossians 2:19). The author's concern, due to rumors of heresy among the Colossians, was to establish without question the lines of authority in the church. This tightening up of the leadership in the church resulted in women being left out of the repetition in Colossians 3:11 of the otherwise complete baptismal formula of Galatians 3:28. Women are instructed to be subject to their husbands (Colossians 3:18), slaves are exhorted to be subject to their masters (Colossians 3:22). The church's experience is therefore channeled by this metaphor into a hierarchical mold in which the Headship of Christ is mirrored by the headship of bishops over pastors, pastors over churches, husbands over wives, parents over children, masters over slaves.

In this view of the church as composed of leaders and followers, the leadership of women came to be regarded as more and more suspect and eventually became a mark of groups considered sectarian or heretical such as the Montanists and Priscillianists.

Clement, bishop of Rome, admonished the Corinthians that women were to "remain in the rule of subjection" to their husbands precisely at the time when the struggle with gnostic, deemed heretical, Christians was taking place.[10] Irenaeus was aghast at the participation of women in heretical groups. He described the followers of a local gnostic teacher, Marcus, as "many foolish women." Marcus prayed to a "Grace," to her "who is before all things," and to Wisdom and Silence, feminine elements in the Godhead. Marcus allowed women to prophesy and to celebrate the eucharist with him.[11]

Tertullian was another church father who strenuously objected to women's leadership. He argued that teaching, baptism, and offering the eucharist were "masculine functions" and exclaimed in disgust over the audacity of "these heretical women" who taught, engaged in argument, and perhaps even baptized.[12]

Authority in the Christian community came to be vested in a few designated leaders, and these exclusively male. Female leadership became suspect because it denied headship.

A Royal Priesthood, the Bulwark of Truth

The later letters reflect the struggle of the communities with issues of authority, a struggle that resulted in the subordination of women and their exclusion from leadership in the community. This is nowhere clearer than in the domestic codes,[13] a series of exhortations to obedience in the households of the early Christian communities. These appear in 1 Peter and 1 Timothy.

In these epistles, the church is imaged as a "royal priesthood [1 Pet. 2:9]," "the pillar and bulwark of the truth [1 Tim. 3:15]." Likewise, the domestic codes, side by side with these images, reinforce hierarchy and exclusion. Women are instructed to "be submissive to your husbands [1 Pet. 3:1]," servants to "be submissive to your masters [1 Pet. 2:18]," and all to "be subject for the Lord's sake to every human institution, whether it be to the emperor as supreme, or to governors as sent by him [1 Pet. 2:13-14]." Women are to "learn in silence with all submissiveness," and to exercise no authority over men (1 Timothy 2:11, 12). Slaves are to obey masters (1 Timothy 6:1), and all obey deacons and bishops.

Wayne Meeks has observed that women in Corinth understood Galatians 3:28 as modifying their role in society.[14] Schroeder and Crouch contends that the domestic codes were used to repress social unrest within the church among Christian slaves and wives, unrest stimulated by that baptismal formula.[15]

The church in its earliest years was subject to "slanders" on account of its new-found freedom, especially as this was reflected in the behavior of Christian wives and slaves. It may be that the domestic codes reflect not only pressures internal to the communities, but external pressures as well. Pagan households were upset when subordinates became Christians and behaved more freely. Governors of the whole political fabric became concerned. Hence, as a defensive action, Christians were instructed to conform to accepted social custom. This could not help but be reflected in the church's self-definition and the more hierarchical and closed imagery that accompanied it.

The metaphors of the Body of Christ and the New Creation came out of and in turn speak to the earliest church's experience of the newness of life that Christ brings. The post-Pentecostal church struggled to hold on to this vision, and at the same time to survive in the larger culture. Metaphors of Headship, Priesthood, and Bulwark reflect this tension. Increasingly, the church's self-definition becomes tied to accommodation to culture, and the metaphors show this.

THE MEDIEVAL CHURCH

THE medieval church can really be said to begin with the peace of Constantine, because it is with this era that the close attachment between the state and the Christian religion, the hallmark of medieval Christianity, begins. It became legal to leave money to the church, and the church thus began a long period of acquisition that made it a rich and powerful political institution. As Hans Küng has said, "This was worse than a persecution." The church was invaded from within by cultural accommodation, an attack almost irresistible to the band who had struggled with the persecutions of the first three centuries.

One of the important factors that must be taken into account in describing the medieval church is the elaboration of the hierarchy. As noted above, Scroggs points out that the lack of a hierarchy was a striking characteristic of some parts of the earliest church. The development of a complex hierarchy is a hallmark of both the chronological and conceptual stages of the church. Metaphors for the church in use during this period reflect both this development and criticism of it.

The City of God

Yves Congar, in his book on the ecclesiology of the high Middle Ages, observes that it is undoubtedly less accurate to speak of *Kirchenbegriff* (church doctrine) than to speak of *Kirchenbild* (church metaphor) in the high Middle Ages.[16] Social and political metaphors abound, such as the City of God, Jerusalem, and the Temple.[17]

In the year 413, the fertile mind of the then bishop of Hippo, Augustine, began to formulate a response to the detractors of Christianity who claimed that the barbarian invaders from the North were gaining a foothold because of the weakening influence of Christianity within the Roman Empire. His response took more than thirteen years and resulted in the twenty-two books of the *City of God*. The first ten books answer the claim that Christianity is a harmful social and political influence. In the last twelve books, the theme is a description of the rise, progress, and destiny of the two cities.

The two cities are the realities formed by two loves. Earthly love of the self, which can even lead to contempt for God, forms the earthly city. The heavenly city is formed by the love of God, and may even lead to contempt for the self.[18]

There has always been some understandable confusion as to the relationship of the church to the heavenly city, the City of God. In an exposition of Psalm 8, Augustine identifies the City of God with the church: "That city of God is called Zion, the Church, therefore, is Zion."[19] But it is not at all clear that for Augustine himself this metaphor was always related to the existential church. The distinction he makes between the two cities is too absolute to correspond completely to two earthly institutions.[20]

Nevertheless, it has been significant for the history of Christianity that Augustine chose a social and political image for his work. The combination of a social and a religious image meant to later theologians that the church would come to dominate the earthly society. This gave the church enormous political power. But in contrast to the New Creation image of the New Testament period, in this view of the church, social distinctions are not abolished when brought into the City of God. When the City of God is interpreted as the church, it is, on the contrary, "so far from rescinding and abolishing these diversities, [that it] even preserves and adopts them, so long only as no hindrance to the worship of the one supreme and true God is thus introduced."[21]

The maintenance of diversities leads to greater harmony in life and is, therefore, necessary to "the perfectly ordered and harmonious enjoyment of God and of one another in God."[22] Order is a key category for Augustine. Disorder is virtually equivalent to evil.[23] The peace that comes from the tranquility of order is the highest good.

Women were regarded by Augustine as inferior to men, although he did not rail at them as did some of his contemporaries. The inequality of women requires their exclusion from leadership positions to maintain good order in the church as in the society.

The City of God is a rigidly stratified metaphor that came to be interpreted by those who followed Augustine as a legitimation of inequalities in leadership and decision making in the earthly church.

The Perfect Society

Another social metaphor is the Perfect Society, an image used by Thomas Aquinas and Gregory I (590-604). Building on the Augustinian theme of order, this view regards the church as perfecting and divinely ordaining the stratifications of society.

This ordering was perhaps most visible in the existence of a priestly caste, which became marked after the peace of Constantine. The priesthood, an element in effecting salvation, is regarded as a superior state of being. Women were viewed by the architects of this priestly caste as not even requisitely on a par with men (the human), let alone with priests. In several ecclesiastical canons of the period an argument was made for the necessity of a male priesthood, stating that "the weak should be saved by the strong," women being the former.

St. John Chrysostom, the theorist of the priesthood, may be taken as representative. In homilies on the texts of the domestic codes, Chrysostom developed the theme that from the moment of creation man enjoyed a greater dignity and a primacy over woman. The effect of woman's role in the fall was to turn this primacy of man's into authority. It was not valid to restrict this treatment to Eve, as all women were weak and fickle.[24]

Evidently, then, women were unsuited for the priesthood.[25] But it is also clear that the male layperson was not in a much better condition vis-à-vis the means of salvation. The professionalization of the clergy resulted, unsurprisingly, in a widening gulf between clergy and laity. In the celebration of the mass the clergy stood, the laity knelt. Wine was withheld from the laity with increasing frequency. Lines of authority were drawn in a top-down style.

If the laywoman found herself at the bottom of this pyramid, at the pinnacle stood the pope. After Leo the Great, who connected the papacy directly to Peter, perhaps the real architect of the papacy was Gregory I. Gregory believed that Christian society should reflect heavenly society. As heaven was hierarchical, each soul in its proper place, so should be Christendom. Augustine and Aquinas argued for just such an ordering. Gregory continued in this vein, insisting on a chain of command linking priest to bishop to pope. Jeffrey Russell observes that "notions of hierarchical order became the basis of the unified and structured organization of the Church that progressed from the eighth century and culminated in the political theories of Gregory VII in the eleventh."[26]

Leo the Great had argued for the divine character of the priesthood (176 Ep. XIV, 1, Ep. LXV, 2). But this divinity characterized all ministries of bishops and priests, which were valid insofar as they participated in the communion of the universal bishop (pope) with Christ. All were connected in a great spiritual chain in which the power flowed in one direction only. This organic and visible chain of command was the medieval church.

Obviously the church's self-image changed under such circumstances. The official metaphors in use during the early, middle, and late Middle Ages reflect this change in the church and present an image of an institution increasingly stratified and powerful, dominating the society around it.

The function of the Christian community was not to seek to eliminate inequalities between members, but to underline them for the peaceful function of the whole. A church that functioned with these images would see in its hierarchy an orderly furthering of the peace of God. This type of tightly pyramidal understanding became exclusive, as in practice it was used to justify the maintenance and furtherance of the power of the upper reaches of the chain of command.

The Poor

In the eleventh and twelfth centuries came a great outpouring of religious enthusiasm that was not representative of measure, form, and order. These movements, while difficult to categorize as a whole, represented a desire on the part of all classes to humanize religion, as seen in the veneration of Mary, and in some way to regain control over their own religious lives.

Many of these groups focused on living out the virtues of simplicity and poverty, values not overly stressed in the upper reaches of the medieval church. The epithet "the Poor" was specifically applied to some of these groups, and is used here to represent the image to which these groups sought to recall the church.

The Old Testament frequently describes the righteous in Israel as the poor. In the later second century a Jewish-Christian group, the Ebionites, may have adopted "the Poor" as a title for the church.[27] The Gospel of Luke is filled with imagery of the poor, and there is frequent identification of the disciples with the poor. Were the disciples called "the Poor," and was this ever an early self-image of the church? Rosemary Ruether interprets these images in Luke to mean that "the primary identity of the people of God ceases to be taken, symbolically, from the ruling classes, i.e., sons and princes. Instead, the primary identity of the people of God comes from the poor and despised, women and slaves."[28]

The concept of the *vita apostolica*, from the time of the Gregorian Reform, was rooted in three fundamentals: imitation of the primitive church, poor, simple, and humble; a love of souls; and evangelical poverty and the common life. Although associated with monasticism, its appeal was largely to laypersons, and to a great extent to laywomen.[29]

Researchers into this widespread religious movement have frequently remarked on the extent of the response of women to these newer modes of religious life. The foundational work of Herbert Grundmann suggests that the extent of women's participation may indicate that they were influential in shaping the idea of the *vita apostolica*, rather than merely following ideas that had been generated by men alone.[30]

To begin with, this influx of women and their enthusiasm was greeted warmly not only by the reformers of the monastic orders, but also by mendicant preachers of the idea of poverty and mission to the world in imitation of Christ and the apostles.

But as increasing numbers of women sought inclusion, the reformed orders began to refuse to admit them. The mounting conflict between these orders and the large numbers of women aspiring to religious perfection resulted in a movement of women who, although not constituting an order, endeavored without public vows to promote among their members a life of Christian perfection. These women, known as the Beguines, were found throughout Europe during the high Middle Ages.

Because this movement was loosely connected and varied in form, it is difficult to define.[31] The Beguines were for the most part poor women or widows who lived together for economic as well as spiritual reasons. In fact, the Beguine movement has been studied as part of the analysis of the *Frauenfrage* in the Middle Ages.[32] It is significant that some Beguines thought of themselves as the mothers of the poor.[33]

Thirteenth-century conciliar legislation reflects a rapidly growing concern of the ecclesiastical authorities over the proliferation of these Beguine communities. A common charge made against the Beguines was mendicancy, though it can be shown that the movement did not regularly foster mendicancy as much as experiments in communal living and working.[34]

Another criticism was the absence of regular condition, a nonformalized life-style. Alongside this critique is found the suspicion of "novelties," whose possibilities provoked the wrath of Guillaume de Saint-mour, whom Ernest McDonnell calls "that ardent champion of the hierarchy inviolate." As McDonnell points out, "Back of his charges of hypocrisy may be discerned hostility to competition with established prerogative."[35]

The established clergy did, in fact, seem to perceive in the Beguines a threat to their power in preaching and teaching, and with good cause. Vernacular preaching and biblical translation were the ultimate outcome of this reform movement. It stressed voluntary obedience, and remained informal despite pressures to conform to established practice and be subject to local clerical authority. It can be described, with care, as a democratization of religious experience, with an emphasis on equal participation and responsibility. As such, it was rightly perceived as a menace to the heavenly city, the Perfect Society, with the images of established privilege these represented.

The Beguine movement eventually succumbed in the usual way of reform movements. Its more radical expressions disappeared, and the rest were incorporated into the larger church, with some small impact on that institution. The Beguines represented a protest within the religious life of women, and of the laity in general, against practices of exclusion within the church. The metaphor that best expresses the self-image of this movement is the Poor, because these movements were a direct challenge to those self-understandings of the medieval church that were taken from the ruling classes and employed by the "princes" of the church.[36] The primary identity of the People of God, according to the Beguines, is with the poor.

The medieval church was a place of striking contrasts, and the metaphors used to describe it demonstrate this. On the one hand, the church hierarchy, increasingly closed and authoritarian, used metaphors that describe the church as a ruling political force. The laity, on the other hand, described their protests against this rigidity with the metaphor of the Poor, an image that captures the essence of what it means to be out of power in the world.

AMERICAN PROTESTANTISM IN THE NINETEENTH CENTURY

THE next period of the church to be examined needs careful analysis. Unlike the two previous periods, in America in the nineteenth century there were no dominant metaphors for the church.

Between the fifteenth century and the nineteenth, the Reformation caused a break in the supposed universality of the church, and modern thought challenged its supposed eternality. It may be that the absence of metaphor is due to these upheavals. But it must be stressed that the Protestant Church in particular has never attained a strong sense of itself, of which the absence of metaphor gives evidence. But there are some designations for the church to be found during this period, and these must form the basis for renewed assessment of the church.

Denominations

While Protestantism may be described as a sect type for the most part, in contrast to the medieval church type (Troeltsch)[37] of Catholicism, this must be qualified for American Protestantism, especially in the nineteenth century and later. In the nineteenth century a new type appeared, the denomination.

A denomination represented both church-type and sect-type characteristics in a way that had not been seen before in the history of the church.

The denomination resembles the church type in that it is intimately related to the world. The mighty of the society are the prominent members of the churches, as the kings, dukes, and earls of an earlier period were significant in the medieval church. These leading laity are very much in the world. They transact business, wage war, and play with no thought that these pursuits contradict their religious principles.

Yet the modern American denomination also retains sectarian elements. There is almost no authority to the clerical office. Lay participation is strong, if not, in fact, dominant. There is almost no objective holiness of sacrament, liturgy, or doctrine; their significance is the degree to which they call up an inner witness.[38]

The denomination, like the sect, exhibits little interest in a sacred hierarchical ecclesiastical system, but the denominational hierarchy is very much in evidence and as closely knit as any found in the high Middle Ages. Even in denominations whose theological predilections are against institutional structure, there is great emphasis on the growth of the institution itself.

This curious turn of events underlines the extent to which the American Protestant Church's actual experience of itself is cut off from the predominant metaphors, either inclusive or exclusive, that have been in force in the past. This church's understanding of what it means to be a church comes largely from outside itself and represents a break between images or metaphors and experience.

The idea of the church represented by the word denomination gained currency not coincidentally at the same time that Protestant churches underwent disestablishment in America, a most traumatic event. Disestablishment was the process that terminated state support for certain religious groups: Congregationalism in Connecticut and Massachusetts, Episcopalianism in Virginia and New York, Presbyterianism in New Jersey. These had enjoyed hegemony over other groups who were not so established. When Congregationalism was disestablished in Massachusetts in 1833, the process was complete.

Churches were forced to become voluntary associations, a process begun in American thought long before it was accomplished in legal practice. Religion was being cut off from the public, political sphere and confined to personal values and conduct. This was the result not only of a general democratization, which decreed that no one religious group should have automatic precedence over any other, but also was produced by the competitive, commercial spirit of industrialization, which challenged the values of the Christian gospel and decreed them inapplicable to business.

The churches were able to retain some authority, but it was retained at a price. The price was the independent identity of religion as against culture. Religion triumphed in America by identifying with and upholding American values. Thus Sydney Mead writes:

> At the time Protestantism in America achieved its greatest dominance of the culture, it had also achieved an almost complete ideological and emotional identification with the burgeoning bourgeois society and its free-enterprise system, so that "in 1876 Protestantism presented a massive, almost unbroken front in its defence of the social *status quo*."[39]

Hence, there is a sense in which "denomination" means nothing. It is, as Martin Marty points out, "a studiously neutral term, a 'nothing' or noncommittal word." It means, simply, category. Churches, however, like to think of themselves as *Church,* and all other groups as sects or cults. But on the American scene, churches were forced to accept denomination as their label if they wished to remain within "society's legal pattern of toleration."[40]

This precarious existence explains the exclusivity of denominations with regard to women.

Protestant churches were not the only group disestablished by industrialization. During the nineteenth century, industrialization eliminated the active, productive role that women had played in colonial home industry. Dispossessed from productivity, the middle-class white woman in the nineteenth century was identified with the virtues of a glorified domesticity because a support structure was needed to raise children and meet the needs of the absentee industrial (male) worker.[41]

Women and religion were both domesticated—that is, relegated to the private sphere. Yet it is logical that while ministers were associated with the feminine sphere of home and hearth, they should be the first to criticize women who abandoned this sphere. Ministers had much to lose if women abandoned their proper sphere. As Ann Douglas states the case, "Clerical hostility [toward women's advancement was a form] of territorial imperative springing from an uneasy sense of a too cramped common space."[42] Ministers dared not be identified in a wholly feminine role or, they believed, they would lose whatever authority remained to the religious enterprise. They were among the first to exclude women from leadership.

An example of this exclusive attitude on the part of the nineteenth-century Protestant denominational ministers toward women is the missions movement. The first women to participate in the missionary movement were wives of male missionaries. They went along to care for their husbands and to "protect" them from the temptations of savages.[43] The missionary wife was frequently more accepted in the local life via her relationships to the other women. During their first five years in Burma, Adoniram Judson did not make a single male convert, but Ann Judson met regularly during this period with twenty to thirty women.[44] This success, however, was wholly within women's proper sphere.

Almost no single women were permitted to go overseas as missionaries until the time of the Civil War. Protestant women at home were largely responsible for supporting single woman missionaries through the development of women's boards of mission, which raised funds and disseminated information about missions. These missionary societies or missionary boards functioned as auxiliaries to the male-dominated denominational boards of mission. While these women's societies carried on a wide variety of activities, the women sponsoring them refrained from speaking publicly in mixed gatherings and sought permission for any major policy program or budget change. Yet, even so, their work met with great resistance and often with outright opposition.[45] Insofar as women's boards of mission were tolerated, they were forced to be separate and submit to male direction.

Nevertheless, women's missions grew until in 1888 there were more women, both single and married, in missions than men. The limits on women's activity were reasserted strenuously by the secretary of the American Baptist Missionary Union.

> While it must be accepted as the duty of single ladies to be helpful in all departments of the work, it ought to be expected of them that they will carefully abstain from any interference with matters not specially committed to their hands. Women's work in foreign fields must be careful to recognize the headship of man in ordering the affairs of the Kingdom of God. We must not allow the major vote of the better sex, nor the ability and efficiency of so many of our female helpers, nor even the exceptional faculty for leadership and organization which some of them have displayed in their work, to discredit the natural and predestined headship of man in Missions, as well as in the Church of God: "Adam was first formed, then Eve," and "the head of the woman is the man." This order of creation has not been changed by Redemption, and we must conform all our plans and policies for the uplifting of the race through the power of the Gospel to this Divine ordinance.[46]

Exclusion of women from the highest levels of leadership and from decision-making roles is necessary for denominational leaders to retain a sense of authority vis-à-vis the larger culture. This culture sought to identify both women and religion as belonging to the private sphere and hence to devalue their contributions to society. Denominations could not risk any further devaluation, and opposed women's leadership.

The ultimate fate of women's mission boards illustrates this point. By the beginning of the twentieth century, the women's boards had achieved great success in the missions effort. While still under denominational auspices, their activities were becoming more independent as their outreach and their fund raising expanded. During the early twentieth century, women's mission groups faced a concerted attack on their independence by the denominations, and were forced, one by one, to become integrated into the general boards. Promises of representation and leadership roles were made in negotiations, but rarely, if ever, became reality. Sometimes the denominational leaders did not even trouble to negotiate: in 1922 the Presbyterian General Assembly voted to merge the Women's Board of Foreign Mission with the Board of Mission without consulting either group.[47]

After the dissolution of women's boards, women missionaries were gradually outnumbered by men. A generation of women leaders disappeared as denominations replaced them with men. The ranks closed in order to serve whatever tenuous identity the denominations could achieve in American society.

Sectarian Protestantism

Sydney Ahlstrom has called the first half of the nineteenth century "sectarian heyday."[48] This is the same period in which Douglas has identified the "feminization" of American culture, which resulted in the privatization of women and religion. These two phenomena are not unrelated. Sects challenged the prevailing cultural values. One sign of the challenge was the strikingly prominent role women played in sectarian leadership. Furthermore, these sects tended to employ metaphors to describe their experience, where mainline denominations did not.

The United Society of Believers in Christ's Second Coming, the Shakers, was founded and led in America by a woman, Ann Lee. The Shakers were deliberately countercultural in their forms and frequently imaged their communal experience with the metaphor of the New Creation.

Ann Lee was ultimately regarded by her followers as a second messiah, the female counterpart of Jesus of Nazareth. In 1806, Benjamin S. Youngs, an elder in the Shaker Church, published *The Testimony of Christ's Second Coming*. He argued for the idea of a Godhead composed of Father, Son, Holy Mother Wisdom, and Daughter. This view became doctrine in the sect.[49]

> All life and activity animated by Christian Love is Worship. Shakers adore God as the Almighty Creator, Fountain of all Good, Life, Light, Truth and Love,—the One Eternal Father-Mother.
>
> They recognize the Christ Spirit, the expression of Deity, manifested in fulness in Jesus of Nazareth, also in feminine manifestation through the personality of Ann Lee, both, they regard as Divine Saviors, anointed Leaders in the New Creation. All in whom the Christ consciousness awakens are Sons and Daughters of God.[50]

This perspective provided the root for their communitarian and egalitarian life together imaged by the New Creation. There is a genuinely new, if not radical, form evident in Shaker life. Sexual intercourse was considered to be at the root of sin and was abandoned. Shakers participated in a communal life that stressed ideals of simplicity, celibacy, and equality.[51]

Ann Lee was not the only strong female leader of the sect. Lucy Wright became the leader of the central Shaker ministry in 1796 and presided over a period of great expansion of the sect. She was particularly interested in new forms of worship and added songs, dances, and unison marches to the already unusual Shaker worship experience.

Also founded by a woman, Christian Science is another sectarian movement begun during this period. Mary Baker Eddy, a sickly woman, found physical relief in the contemplation of an infinite spirit. "All consciousness is Mind," she wrote, "and Mind is God."[52] Overcoming evils, both physical and spiritual, is a matter of recognition of the oneness of mind in God.

Healed of her infirmity by this belief, she shared her discovery with others and in 1879 the organization was chartered as The Church of Christ (Scientist). When the church was reorganized in 1892 under a self-perpetuating board of directors, Mrs. Eddy was designated pastor emeritus and retained control until her death.[53]

Mrs. Eddy encouraged women's leadership and was an important backer of the women's suffrage movement. Women in Christian Science, under her guidance, were encouraged to become readers and practitioners. Augusta Emma Simmons Stetson eventually became a leader of a rival branch of Christian Science in New York City and challenged Mrs. Eddy's authority. Christian Science has retained visible and important female leadership.[54]

In Christian Science God is imaged in feminine terms. In her magnum opus, *Science and Health: With Key to the Scriptures (1875)*, Mrs. Eddy wrote: "In divine science we have not as much authority for considering God masculine, as we have for considering Him feminine, for Love imparts the clearest idea of Deity."[55]

The church is also imaged in feminine terms. There is one Mother Church of Christian Science in Boston. Other churches of Christian Science are termed branches. The church is referred to in Mrs. Eddy's writing as Mother.

There is a striking contrast between the absence of metaphorical language for the church in denominational writings and the presence of metaphor in sectarian communities. A sense of self is gained in the latter only by conscious repudiation of the dominant culture. Likewise, a sense of self is lost, as evidenced by the absence of metaphor, in the dominant denominations through cultural accommodation. Accommodation to the dominant culture by mainline Protestant denominations is illustrated by their exclusive practices toward women, whereas sectarian women's leadership demonstrates a break with the larger culture.

As twentieth-century Protestantism struggles toward self-definition, both these insights are crucial. The flat and nearly antiecclesiological language of much of American Protestantism both reflects and permits the cultural accommodation so typical of American Protestantism. Yet the historical survey also reveals that metaphors for the church can draw the church out toward renewed self-awareness.

Women's experience in the church provides the key to the next steps. The Inclusive Church is the New Creation, the Body of Christ, the Poor, the Mother Church. These inclusive metaphors that speak of women's experience point the way for American denominations to overcome their insularity and can help them to become more inclusive representatives of Christ in history.

Chapter 2 METAPHORS FOR THE CONTEMPORARY CHURCH

IN THE last decade, Latin American theologians of liberation have had enormous impact on the church in North America, as well as South America. The work of the Latin American theologians of liberation in regard to the church is a serious force in discussions of the renewal of the church in North America.

In addition, the Latin American theologians of liberation have greatly influenced the thought of some North American feminists; their work is one crucial root of this study. They have taught that Christians can no longer talk about the "unity of the Body of Christ" and ignore the fact of the disunity of the churches. We have learned that we cannot begin to talk about the equality of the New Creation until we have examined the inequalities of power distribution in the institutional churches. We know now that we cannot understand such equality until we have struggled to rectify inequality. The Latin Americans have shown us that the church is the starting point for contemporary ecclesiology.

But when that injunction is taken seriously, important differences are seen between the churches of North and South America. Metaphors that emerge out of each context will need to be examined for their applicability to the other.

Latin American Christendom

IT is crucial to remember that Latin America is primarily a Catholic context and must be so understood. As was discussed in the previous chapter, the Perfect Society and the City of God are two Roman Catholic metaphors used for the church. This is the origin of what has been called the "Christendom" mentality, the view that the world is contained by the church.

The Roman Catholic Church has centuries of practical experience of this universality. The church has dominated the Western world. This situation was challenged, clearly, in the Reformation of the sixteenth century. But, in the narrowed Northern and Western world view, one tends to forget that this challenge was rather confined. Latin America did not experience the Reformation as it was experienced in Europe. It was, in fact, primarily colonized by those who were part of the Counter-Reformation, who were passionately pro-Christendom, so to speak.

The Kingdom of God

Christendom is not extinct in Latin America; it forms one crucial part of that situation. But another view emerged from within the Roman Catholic Church in recent years, an attempt to understand and accommodate the church to the living fact that the unity of social life and the life of faith no longer exists. Jacques Maritain sought to take seriously the church and the world as separate and real entities. There is a "distinction of planes," which dictates that the church and the world contribute to the historical enterprise in distinctly different ways. Yves Congar writes:

> By converting men to faith and baptizing them according to the mission she has received from the Lord, the Church presents and actualized herself as the "older part" of salvation and holiness in the world. By acting in the sphere of civilization, which means in the temporal order and in history, she fulfills her mission to be the soul of human society.[1]

This perspective contributed to the discussion by recognizing the autonomy of the world. It further stimulated genuine social action on the part of its proponents. But apart from certain pastoral circles, this movement did not extend into the greater practice of the church in Latin America. The church in Latin America is so closely tied to the existing social order that the model, when employed, was used to shore up sagging social institutions.[2]

It was primarily the dawning recognition that the distinction-of-planes model was applied rather discriminatingly in the church that stimulated the Latin American theologians of liberation to move beyond it. It became apparent to them that the principle of distinction is "not applied when it is a question of maintaining the status quo, but it is wielded when, for example, a lay apostolic movement or group of priests hold an attitude considered subversive to the established order."[3] It thus became clear that the church is able, through this distinction, to maintain strong ties to the power elites in the world and at the same time "to preach a lyrical spiritual unity of all Christians."[4]

The distinction-of-planes model is radicalized by the theologians of liberation with the metaphor of the Kingdom of God. The church and the world are unified, as each can contribute to the Kingdom of God in its own way. The Kingdom of God is the reality of God's action in history, to which the church must conform and beside which the church is nothing. This metaphor effectively overcomes the separation cf history in the distinction-of-planes model, but counters the Christendom mentality, because the world belongs not to the church but to God.

The Kingdom of God is further radicalized by an eschatological vision tied to the existing social order and becomes in Leonardo Boff's phrase, "The Utopia of Absolute Liberation."[5] Utopia means the earth, precisely the idea these theologians mean to convey. Yet they also recognize that no movement for liberation in history can ever fully realize God's intention for history. Utopia, therefore, retains a future orientation that is a fulfillment gratuitously given by God and only by God.[6]

The Poor

While the metaphors of Utopia or the Kingdom of God provide the stance from which to criticize the institutional church for its failure of justice, the metaphor of the Poor is employed to change the structures themselves.

Another context for Latin America is that millions are on the borderline of starvation. Nearly one-half its population suffers from infectious diseases. Two-thirds, if not more, of the agricultural, forest, and live-stock resources in Latin America are controlled or owned by a handful of persons and corporations.[7] Governmental repression of social unrest caused by these conditions has accelerated as leadership has become increasingly drawn from the military after successive overthrows of popular regimes.

In response to this crisis, the theologians of liberation in Latin America have opted for the identification of the church with the poor. In contrast to critics who note that the "option" for the poor at the heart of Latin American theologies of liberation creates an identity crisis for the church, appearing to pull the church into the world, these theologians assert that this option is not outside the church's essential being, but at its center. The option for the poor, they claim, is not a human assertion, but the choice of God. It is God's choice as witnessed in the life and death of Jesus who was called the Christ. It is Jesus' identification with the poor and lowly to which the church must "con-form" in order to be the Church of Jesus Christ.[8]

Thus the intolerable conditions in Latin America of widespread poverty and starvation must be of primary concern to the church, since the church is the poor themselves. This view does not abandon one plane for another, but recognizes the unity of history and the church's being in it.

Father Rutilio Grande was the first of seven priests murdered in El Salvador in 1977. He had a vision of the church organized in small communities that would focus the gospel around the problems of the people and focus their efforts toward improving their lives. "God is not in the clouds, lying in a hammock," he proclaimed, "but is at work and wants you to build the kingdom here on earth."⁹

After four years of work, twenty-seven such small groups had sprung up in Aquilaries, twenty miles north of San Salvador. Three hundred *anamators* or lay leaders took turns directing the communities. When a dispute broke out over the intolerable wages paid to the sugar cane cutters, $3 per day, Grande was able from the base of these communities to lead a strike, which the workers won. He was murdered on March 12, 1977.

During his funeral procession, in which hundreds of peasants walked in the blistering heat to the graveside, one priest explained, "This is truly the people's church. The bishops' meeting at Puebla was important in determining whether the bishops belong to this church. The fact is, the bishops need this church."¹⁰ This new church of the people, proclaimed at Grande's funeral, is understood as the "sacrament of history," the place where the grace of God in Christ is active, helping people to "take their dignity into their hands," no longer waiting "fatalistically for happiness in the life beyond."¹¹ Bishops of the institutional church, if they do not act in this church, can cease to be identified as part of the Body of Christ on earth.

Thus arise the basic Christian communities, or BCCs, small groups of Christians, largely lay led, who share the responsibilities of life equally and who combine a deep spirituality with a heightened political consciousness. Spirituality and consciousness-raising are not two phenomena, separate parts of the community life, but are joined in one vision. As Grande is reported to have said, BCCs seek "a more human and a more just world in which all Salvadorans may be able to share the goods, seated at the common table of the creation, just as we share at this Eucharist table."

Rosemary Ruether has described the basic Christian community.

> There are many small groups whose focus remains the interior life—prayer meetings, Bible study groups, charismatic meetings—and who adopt no stance of social criticism or action and are even resistant to it. In its present usage, the basic Christian community . . . does not include these types of groups. Rather, it refers specifically to that type of small, committed Christian community that seeks to unite theological and biblical reflection with social analysis leading to action for justice. Liberation theology, with its interconnection of praxis and theological reflection, then, is constitutive of those groups here called basic Christian communities.[12]

These small groups find the Bible central to their life together. But they are committed not simply to Bible study, but to Bible praxis, the effort to reflect on the political realities that shape their members' lives in light of the scriptures and to organize for change in that light. These groups must, perforce, be able to define their own tasks and must not be controlled from the outside.

The impact of the BCCs on ecclesiology in Latin America is assessed differently, depending on the situation in the church of the assessor. At the bishops' meeting in Puebla, Mexico, in February of 1979, basic communities were hailed as a priority for the church and described as "the focal point of evangelization, the motor of liberation." In this view, while the basic Christian communities are important, their task within the parishes is evangelization. For members of these communities, and for the theologians of liberation in Latin America, however, BCCs represent an entirely different approach to the whole doctrine of the church.

When Vatican Council II emphasized the church as the people of God, this softened the language of *Magisterium* and was perceived by some to mean that the church hierarchy was not in fact the church. Basic Christian communities most radically incarnate this change. The church arises not from the top down, but from the bottom up. The church then exists where these local gatherings meet in equality and learn from each other what it means to be human in the eyes of God.

The New Creation

Another way of describing the basic Christian community is with the metaphor of the New Creation. Participants in basic Christian communities "believe that the Holy Spirit has been poured out on all, and all have a voice. This view of equality has led to a redefinition of authority and placed the responsibility to preach Christ on every member of the community."[13] The language causes one almost irresistibly to think of the New Testament use of the title the New Creation. The newness of life in Christ is visible in the life together of the BCCs.

Thus leadership has begun to be extended to women, although in Latin America it has not been possible to raise women's equality as an issue to any great extent. Women's groups in Buenos Aires, Argentina, are forced to meet in secret, and at least one such gathering has been broken up by the police. Yet despite these obstacles, some women's leadership is reported.

In Italy, where women's traditional situation has not been one of equality, basic Christian communities have a specifically feminist thrust. At the fourth National Congress of the Basic Christian Community Movement in Italy held in Naples in 1977 (the first was in Rome in 1971), women obtained a place on the agenda to address the problems faced by women active both in the feminist movement and in BCCs. The commission report that came out of the congress pointed out that while feminism and faith in Christ are ideally to be seen as "life styles which lead to liberation and not as two ideologies which are counterposed to each other," within the feminist movement "many sisters . . . tend to identify us [Christian women] with the institutional structures of the Church." This has led to a study of the ideology of the institutional church, and a recognition that it is the institutionalized aspects of the church which must be fought, as they promote "mystifying values about our [women's] role in society."[14]

This salutary development in Italy may prefigure the same identification between women's liberation and the liberation sought through basic Christian communities. The Mexican organization Women for Dialogue met in October 1979 to reflect on "The Latin American Woman: The Praxis and Theology of Liberation." In the final document to come out of that seminar, the women identified their own struggles with patriarchy and with the struggles of all the oppressed in Latin America, out of which have come the BCCs. These women noted "Women's presence in the construction of Christian communities of the common people, but the absence of any theological reflection that incorporates the women's question." They called for women's leadership in the BCCs and declared that "every theologian of liberation should be urged to reformulate his or her theological categories from a women's standpoint, and to explore revelation more deeply from the same standpoint."[15]

Basic Christian communities, at least to an outsider, share many characteristics with the earliest Christian communities. They are sectarian in ethos, open in terms of membership and decision-making style (increasingly with reference to women), and a source of new life for their members. The novelty of this kind of experience, a genuinely new thing happening in history, is that to which the metaphor of the New Creation speaks. The newness of the way the members of these basic Christian communities relate to one another reflects the fact of the act of God in Christ, a New Creation. This novelty contrasts sharply with the old way of doing things. The old order is slavishly subject, fearful of its own liberation. The new order attempts to grasp the newness that is already present in our midst, as, for example, women and men in these groups struggle with the equality of women.

Basic Christian communities challenge the ecclesiology of the Latin American Church precisely because these churches participate in the Christendom mentality. Phillip Berryman, in an article on basic Christian communities, comments: "I have limited myself to Catholic [BCCs] for several reasons: Catholics are the overwhelming numerical majority and the Catholic Church as an institution is inevitably an important social force, while Protestant churches in general have the status of private associations."[16] The Catholic Church in Latin America has a public status and an explicit identification with the ruling powers of these countries, which is effectively challenged by the approach of the basic Christian community.

The Christendom mentality of the predominant Roman Catholic Church in Latin America is subverted by the metaphors of the Kingdom of God or Utopia. History does not belong to the church, but to God. Furthermore, the church itself no longer belongs to the elites, but to the poor themselves. In basic Christian communities the poor experience the New Creation, the new life that Christ brings. The Poor and the New Creation metaphors represent the challenge of Latin American theologies of liberation to contemporary ecclesiology.

NORTH AMERICAN PROTESTANTISM

IT has been asked time and again by North American Christians concerned with social justice questions whether Latin American theologies of liberation are "for export," or whether their insights relate only to the particular situation of Latin America. There is great interest in North America in the model of the basic Christian community.[17] It is seen as a way to renew the church in North America as well. But it is important to consider whether, in a situation that is primarily Protestant, in which the numerical majority find themselves in what Berryman describes as churches that are "private associations," the renewal of the church can come by this model.

Ever since Troeltsch, we have clearly seen that our North American denominational Protestant churches have had many sect-type characteristics and are voluntaristic associations. Denominations are divided from one another. The schismatic character of Protestant churches has allowed the cultural accommodation that occurred in the face of advancing industrialization in the nineteenth century and that is characteristic of Protestant denominationalism. Do we need to fragment ourselves further by copying the Latin American basic Christian community?

The Kingdom of God

An essential point of debate between North American and South American theologians is over the crucial starting place for doing theology. As has already been noted, in the Latin American situation, a division of history into sacred and secular planes cut the nerve of ethical effort in the social realm for Christians. Latin American theologians of liberation, therefore, see the unification of history and the identification of God's history with human struggles for liberation in their countries in the metaphors of the Kingdom of God or Utopia as pivotal for their task.

Frederick Herzog is one white North American theologian who has raised the question of whether this is *the* starting place for North American theologies that seek to take liberation themes seriously. Is North America suffering from a division of the historical task, which must be overcome by a radical identification of the Christian movement with human struggles for liberation? Herzog had been reading Bellah's *The Broken Covenant*, and through his own experiences with another situation, that of black Americans in the Southern United States, had come to be suspicious of the historical task in North America as it was already co-opted by white Americans.

From its earliest roots, America has been an experiment in liberation. In another age and another culture, it is true, but nevertheless, those who first settled these shores perceived themselves to be the agents of God's task in history; the City on the Hill, the New Jerusalem that they built, was to be God's Kingdom on earth.

But almost from the first, the covenant to be God's people was broken in practice. Those who already occupied the American territory were displaced and finally destroyed by those who had made this identification between their history and God's history.[18] Within their society itself, dissent was ruthlessly punished, and the action of the Spirit was confined to the decisions of the body politic. Americans, therefore, have always seen themselves as the Kingdom of God, "one nation under God," but with less stress over the years on the judgment implied by that subordination. We are one people who are right alongside God.

When nineteenth-century Protestantism was disestablished and largely confined to the private sphere by an advancing capitalist economy, liberalism triumphed in theology precisely because it could accommodate itself to culture. Jonathan Edwards could not, and was run out of Northampton in 1750 because he did not, accommodate himself to the values of industrialization. But the liberals survived because they were able to compartmentalize religion and so ride out the capitalist onslaught. The sense of living in God's Kingdom continued, and certainly has been available to us in inaugural address after inaugural address.[19] But without a clear and present public status for religion, the prophetic stance that was at least possible for preachers in their established pulpits during the American Revolution was conspicuously absent during the Vietnam war.[20]

Thus, Herzog has sought a stance outside this mainstream unification of American history and God's history into the Kingdom of God, specifically in order to "confront" white Christian Americans "point blank" with the biblical word.[21] While Hugo Assmann and others argue for a theology whose "'text' is our situation, and seek to make our situation our primary and basic reference point,"[22] in North American liberal Protestantism, our situation is precisely *that from which we dare not take our text.* This is what we have been doing for over two hundred years.

Thus, says Herzog:

> We have to remain utterly critical and see that North America presents a temptation all by itself with the infinite absorptive capacity of capitalism. The Bible, tradition, the teaching authority of the Church, history of dogma, and so on (Assmann) among mainline U.S. Protestants have been subject to extreme ridicule and rejection for years. Several years ago a minister of my denomination told me: "The Bible? We should take the book off the pulpit and shelve it." Capitalism can be so strong in this country because nearly every critical vantage point has either been co-opted or otherwise made innocuous. "Religion," someone from the South said recently, "that's God and the free enterprise system." In the U.S. we do not need to discover that Bible and tradition are not a primary source of truth itself unconnected with truth-in-action. Bible and tradition have already been dissolved into truth-in-capitalist-action. And everyone has become his or her own judge.[23]

Americans need, therefore, to maintain a sharp critical distance when considering the meaning of the Kingdom of God in order to get away from "a doctrine of America's providential destiny to provide an example of equality and democracy to redeem the entire world."[24]

Herzog's analysis appears to obtain for white, mainline American Protestant denominations. But, as was noted in the section on American Protestantism in chapter 1, there are other resources in North America and other experiences of history. A strong American radical religious tradition has explicitly dissented from this identification of American public history with the Kingdom of God. Further, many North Americans have not been privileged to belong to the Kingdom. Blacks, women, Chicanos, Native Americans—all have been denied entry into the spotlight of American official history, and hence already constitute another locus from which to evaluate this theology of glory that is the American experience.[25]

In his work, Herzog comes close to saying that God's Kingdom comes no matter what human beings do about it. He explicitly rejects José Miranda's claim that "a person must regard human history as his only church," Gustavo Gutiérrez's "self-liberation," and Juan Luis Segundo's "notion of this world becoming the new heaven of God."[26] Herzog repeatedly stresses "God's struggle for justice," "God's activity in history," and so forth, as a corrective to the self-centered, ideologically blind character of Protestant liberalism à la Fredrich Schleiermacher.[27] But in the hermeneutic of theologies of liberation, Christians have given up the kind of individualism that made this liberal ignorance so temptingly possible. Theology is no longer a kind of private enterprise done alone in specific professional locales. A solidarity among those who experience oppression and their reflection and action in community can help prevent the kind of manipulation so easily effected in North America to convince us that America is God's Kingdom.

The Body of Christ

One metaphor that speaks to this experience is that of the Body of Christ. Paul used this metaphor to speak to the Corinthians, who were divided and competing over their so-called spiritual gifts. It conveys a structure in which all have different functions, but in which all play an equally important role. This intentionality is true to the basic theological premise of Latin American theologians of liberation, that action gives rise to thought.

Protestants hear about the Body of Christ incessantly, mostly as an excuse for the lack of unity among the actual Protestant churches. We are really already one in Christ, we hear, and hence our existential disunity is not seen for the scandal it really is. But we cannot *understand* what it means to be the Body of Christ until we struggle existentially to incarnate this experience among ourselves. The racially, sexually, and culturally stratified American Protestant Church prevents the metaphor of the Body of Christ from speaking to us.

The ecclesiological question, then, is, how do Christians become the Body of Christ, how do we incarnate Christ among us? Taking our clues, as did some members of the early church, from the ways in which Jesus of Nazareth chose to be in community, we have seen that his style was open in terms of membership and was explicitly egalitarian in power distribution among members. The "Jesus movement," as Robin Scroggs has pointed out, was also rather explicitly countercultural, challenging the power of the religious and political elites.

The metaphor of the Body of Christ comes out of and speaks to the reality of Christians bonding together and exercising authority *in*, not over, community. Ecclesiology begins here, in places where this kind of reality is struggling to be.

In the North American reality we have experienced history as unitary. Liberalism as a privatized enterprise allowed culture to co-opt the title of Kingdom of God. Thus the North American Christian experience is one of fragmentation. If the most radical thing the Latin Americans, facing a Christendom mentality, can do is to talk about the basic Christian community as sect, perhaps the most radical thing Christians could do in North America, facing a sectarian mentality, is to talk about the Church Universal.

But this is not the church universalized. The method of the theologies of liberation has taught that thought moves from the particular to the general. Hence thought about the North American Church Universal must start where glimmers of this type of universality exist. I will argue that it exists in the women's movement in the churches, and in the peace movement.

North American Christians can neither duck the problem of the way the Kingdom of God has been co-opted by American culture, nor can they retreat from the demand of oppressed peoples that *this* history which we all live is the scene of human liberation. North American Christians must struggle to confront the ideology of America as God's Chosen People *while at the same time* affirming that God's acts of liberation occur in community, where we bond together in the struggle for justice and peace. There exists another consciousness in North America besides the dominant, public one.

It is to this consciousness that the metaphor of the Body of Christ can speak. As noted earlier, in describing the reality to which this metaphor points, Paul makes a major ecclesiological statement in 1 Corinthians 13. The way we Christians conduct ourselves in community makes us the Body. If we are jealous or boastful, if we are arrogant because of our superior knowledge and rude to those who do not have our own gifts, if we exercise power and authority over and not *in* community, then we will not embody Christ. At the heart of our ecclesiology, then, is Christ-in-community. In this Christ embodied, "God has so adjusted the body, giving the greater honor to the inferior part, that there may be no discord in the body, but that the members may have the same care for one another [1 Cor. 12:24-25]."

The Poor

The metaphor of the Body of Christ is insufficient for the renewal of the North American Church. Taken by itself, this metaphor can be understood to say that the churches can continue to be marginalized from the mainstream of American culture and privatized, unable to confront this larger culture and call it to task. But the metaphor of the Body of Christ, when combined with the metaphor of the Poor, is radicalized and politicized. This Christ is the Christ for the poor. The Body of this Christ acts out that commitment.

The North American Church also exists in the larger world as context. Two-thirds of the world's population outside the United States is undernourished. With one-fifth of the world's population, the United States consumes one-half of the world's natural resources. This means, broadly speaking, not only that the North American Church is not the poor, but that it is, in fact, enmeshed in a fabric of political and economic oppression which creates poverty. The poor are kept poor so the rest of us can continue to be rich.

Metaphor not only reflects existing reality, it can create it. The metaphor of the Poor can speak to the North American Protestant Church, but it must do so in a different way than in the Latin American Church. The metaphor of the Poor comes as both judgment and challenge to North American Protestants: judgment, because we have failed to have the poor with us always; challenge, because we are to turn from affluence to stand beside the poor in their struggles for social and economic justice.

North American Protestant churches are powerless to effect justice in this time because their self-definition has been dictated by culture. Divided among themselves, they are effectively paralyzed internally and unable to cope in a unified fashion with the challenges to the gospel that the twentieth century presents.

Women and black people play an especially important role in awakening the North American Church to a response to the metaphor of the Poor for the church. Many white women participate in the dual roles of oppressor, as middle-class North Americans, and of oppressed, as part of all women's oppression everywhere. A consciousness of women's oppression can be instrumental in bringing about a sense of solidarity with the oppressions of class and race. These two are part of the oppression of many poor women and women of color.

As a divided church, the white North American Protestant Church needs to hear the metaphor of the Body of Christ for the sake of overcoming denominational insularity. But internally divided along racial, sexual, and class lines, these churches need to hear the metaphor of the Poor as a judgment and a call to public, political action on behalf of the poor and oppressed whom they are called by Christ to advocate.

In bringing about this change in consciousness, women's experience is central to the church. Women, perhaps more than any other oppressed group, have learned that the personal is the political and that the two are inseparable when effecting social change. Women have formed networks across denominational lines and are already working in ecumenical coalitions on their common problems. Further, white women's consciousness of oppression can be a vehicle for the awakening of a consciousness of the interconnectedness of the oppressions of sex, class, and race.

The metaphors of the Body of Christ and the Poor have been available to the church since its earliest centuries. But these metaphors have not been heard for the challenge they bring, because the structure of Christian theology has prevented it. Theologies of exclusion have given us a Christ who divides and a Spirit who comforts but does not challenge.

Chapter 3 A CHRIST FOR THE BODY

CHRISTIANS CANNOT separate their Christology from their practice in the church. Certain Christologies tend to be found with certain forms of the church that are exclusive in practice. Other Christologies appear in changed forms with a church practice that is more inclusive of women and other minorities. Christians have learned that practice gives rise to thought, which in turn changes practice. This entire dynamic is called praxis. A praxis approach to Christology looks at the relationship between what we say about Christ and what we do in the actual, existential church.

A praxis approach to Christology reveals that certain perspectives on Christ operate to effect the unity and cooperation necessary for the Body of Christ metaphor to function, while some Christologies divide and subordinate, subverting the metaphor at its root. The North

American Church needs to be aware of the ways in which traditional Christologies have divided the church and offered some inclusive alternatives.

EXCLUSIVE CHRISTOLOGIES

Messiah of Israel

It has been argued by Rosemary Ruether and others that traditional Christology is fundamentally anti-Semitic.[1] The church's sorry record with regard to the persecution of Jews, most visible in the Holocaust, is directly related to the development of Christology.

The designation of Jesus as the Messiah of Israel on the part of the first-century church is perhaps the first step in the elaboration of a Christian theology. The attempt to co-opt the title of Messiah from Judaism for the martyred hero of this new community or sect meant a considerable struggle with Judaism, which ultimately resulted in Jewish Christians breaking away to form a new group with converts who were not Jewish.

This is the general trend of the development of Christian theology with relation to Jesus as Messiah of Israel. Having named Jesus the long-awaited Messiah of Israel, the early Christian communities were led to expect an imminent end to this order and the instigation at his hand of a new order. When this did not happen, but political conditions worsened instead, Jesus as the Christ was asserted to have *already* triumphed in the spiritual realm, and it was claimed that his future coming would mark the end of time and a heavenly reign.

It was necessary to claim as well that the Jews who did not accept Jesus as Messiah of Israel had not understood this. Jesus as Messiah of Israel in Christian theology necessitates the condemnation of the Jews for their lack of insight.[2] Christians, therefore, deny that Jews have the ability to interpret their own scriptures correctly. The historical events recorded in the "Old" Testament (Hebrew scriptures) are reinterpreted to prefigure Christ and hence lose their historical substance.

This type of exegesis continues today. Certainly the outright hostility of these apologists is gone, but the result of a Christocentric theology is still implicitly to deny the independent integrity of the Jewish scriptures. Thus Gabriel Fackre writes:

> The apostolic testimony to the central acts of the Christian drama, the deliverance wrought in the life, ministry, death, and resurrection of Christ, is the prism through which the light of biblical revelation is to be seen and understood. Thus the *seventy-seven percent* of the Book that is the Hebrew Bible, our Old Testament, is to be understood within its New Testament context. How the law and the prophets are appropriated in the Christian faith is determined by how their promise is illumined and fulfilled in the New Testament.[3]

That type of Christian chauvinism is hardly unusual. Fackre's explanation of how we read our scriptures demonstrates the close relationship between an exclusive focus on the messianic figure of Christ, and a resultant denial of an autonomous Jewish tradition. Christians must find ways to talk about messiahship which make clear that for them, Jesus is the Christ, but which also acknowledge an independent Jewish tradition.

In a presentation to the Association of Professors and Researchers in Religious Education in 1981, Gabriel Moran proposed a route into Jewish-Christian relations. He advocated that Christians stop saying that Christ and the Messiah of Israel are the same.[4] The Messiah of Israel is the expected king and deliverer of the Hebrews. In the life and death of Jesus of Nazareth this concept underwent a decided kenosis, and hence for a Christian to say Jesus is the Christ is not necessarily the same as to say Jesus is the Messiah of Israel.

That theological direction has fueled anti-Semitism. Christ as Messiah of Israel, a crucial step in the development of a specifically Christian theology, also contributed to a viciously exclusive practice by the church in regard to Jews. For nearly two thousand years Christians have scapegoated Jews in order to have the Messiah to themselves. This history must become part of contemporary Christology. It may be that the church needs to admit that Christ is not the Messiah for Israel. This will require much struggle toward redefinition for Christians, but it has the strength of a moral approach to christological reflection.

Bridegroom

Another approach to Christology that has, in practice, resulted in very exclusive practices in the church is the designation of Christ as the Bridegroom of the church, his bride.

Nuptial imagery certainly abounds in both the Hebrew Bible and the New Testament. In the Hebrew Bible the relation between Yahweh and Israel is often compared to that of a Bridegroom and a bride. Hosea and Jeremiah focus on the fidelity of God as Bridegroom to "his" adulterous bride. Both Jewish and Christian interpreters have seen in the Song of Songs an allegory of the relationship between God and "his" people. This appears in the Jewish tradition before the first century C.E., although Jeremias has shown that no Jewish example exists of the Bridegroom imagery being applied to the Messiah.[5]

The application of this image of divine Bridegroom to the Messiah first appears in the New Testament (Matthew 25:1-13; Mark 2:19-20). It is a very prevalent image in the Johannine corpus. John puts himself in the position of "best man" to Christ the Bridegroom: "He who has the bride is the bridegroom; the friend of the bridegroom, who stands and hears him, rejoices greatly at the bridegroom's voice; therefore, this joy of mine is now full [John 3:29]." The impact of this metaphor is clearly to announce Jesus' messiahship, while also understanding the Messiah's divine nature.

In the Pauline epistles, the Bridegroom imagery for Christ is juxtaposed to bridal imagery for the church (2 Corinthians 11:2), the New Israel. Ephesians puts the seal on this androcentric analogy for the relationship between Christ and the church: "Wives, be subject to your husbands, as to the Lord. For the husband is the head of the wife as Christ is the head of the church, his body, and is himself its Savior. As the church is subject to Christ, so let wives also be subject in everything to their husbands [Eph. 5:23-24]."

Contemporary hermeneutics is open to the possibility of taking into account the bias of a patriarchal society in interpreting this passage, hence freeing women from a biblical injunction to be subject to their husbands. While important, this is only half the exegetical work. What then is to be done with the christological half of the analogy?

In order to understand the christological consequences of the Bridegroom/bride imagery, we must look at the way these particular societal designations have functioned. These images appear in the history of theology coupled with a philosophical "chain of being" in which a higher order is deemed more fully real and hence of more value than a lower order.

The use of Aristotelian categories of form and matter, actuality and potentiality, as these were applied to the concepts of maleness and femaleness, resulted in a depreciation not only of women but also of the church. For Aristotle, form and matter were the metaphysical constitutive elements of bodies, but this was matter understood not as a particular physical manifestation, but as the abstract concept of potentiality. Form is that which shapes matter and gives it definition. According to Aristotle, the male supplies the form for the process of conception, the female supplies the matter, since she "lacks soul."[6] In Aristotle's hierarchy of values, it is clearly better to be a provider of form than to be a provider of matter.

Thus the Bridegroom/bride image as applied in medieval scholasticism to the relationship of Christ and the church not only gave divine sanction to the domination of husbands over wives, but had important consequences for understanding Christ's relationship to the church. In a discussion of whether it is appropriate that woman should have been made from man, Thomas Aquinas, not surprisingly arguing in the affirmative, connects the domestic arrangements of medieval life to the association of Christ and the church.

> Because, as the Philosopher says (*Ethics* 8.12), the human male and female are united, not only for generation, as with other animals, but also for the purpose of domestic life, in which each has his or her particular duty, and in which the man is the

head of the woman. Wherefore it was suitable for the woman to be made out of man, as out of his principle. . . . There is a sacramental reason for this. For by this is signified that the Church takes her origin from Christ. Wherefore the Apostle says (Eph. 5:32): *This is a great sacrament; but I speak in Christ and in the Church.*[7]

Women are denied value relative to men in the creation, but so too is the church denied real value by this argument. The devaluation of women and their identification with the church is a deeply rooted problem in ecclesiology that continues today.

This devaluation can be seen especially clearly in the continuation of the Thomist arguments against women's ordination because of their defect in degree, "since it is not possible in the female sex to signify eminence of degree, for a woman is in the state of subjection, it follows that she cannot receive the sacrament of Order."[8]

In a little tract helpfully entitled *Christ and His Bride,* John Saward presents a case for the Church of England against the ordination of women on the premise that the nuptial imagery of Christ and the church is a "bedrock concept" and "is co-extensive with the imagery of sacrifice."[9] The male-predicated uses of God and Christ are not univocal, argues Saward, but indeed "language about God is hierarchically ordered." Male language for God and female language for the church reflects a primary, irreducible mode of discourse and is not a metaphorical, relative use of language.

The images of head and body, of Bridegroom and bride, of Adam and Eve explain both ecclesiology and soteriology in physical/sexual terms, terms hierarchically ordered by the very nature of that to which they refer. Saward agrees with the Vatican Declaration on the Ordination of Women, which concludes:

> Christ is the bridegroom of the Church, whom he won for himself with his blood, and the salvation brought by him is the new covenant; by using this language, revelation shows why the incarnation took place according to the male gender, and makes it impossible to ignore this historical reality.[10]

Women cannot represent the self-giving of the Bridegroom Christ to "his" bride the church, because women lack the gender similarity that makes the sacrifice function, so to speak. The priest "has to have a man's body to play the part of Christ, the God-man."[11]

A number of crucial christological and ecclesiological decisions become visible when this discussion is examined carefully. It is maintained that there is a distinct hierarchy of being in creation. Most notably, the male has more of the "right stuff" (to borrow a phrase from Tom Wolfe) than the female. Further, it is implied that Christ did not become fully human; he merely became male. Maleness is asserted as qualitatively distinct from femaleness—hence the incarnate Christ did not participate in all of humanity. This contradicts an Eastern motto, that what Christ did not assume in the incarnation he did not save. The christological decisions are obviously not unrelated to ecclesiological consequences. The church is asserted to be female, a lower order of being that cannot fully image Christ.

The church is seen under this rubric as a mindless material body, lacking in form. One wonders whether such a passive receptacle can be an agent in history. Is there a role for the church other than blind obedience to male leadership? Who is the church?

Such a hierarchically ordered view of the church effectively paralyzes communal action. It should also be pointed out to the male layperson that under such a rubric he is female in relationship to the church hierarchy. The laity who *are* the people of God are impugned in their capacity to act when they are assigned a stereotyped female role as passive bride.

While in any ultimate sense female leadership is not intrinsically necessary for a change in style (to maintain the contrary would be to buy into the same kind of Aristotelian absolutes), the challenge women's ordination poses to the church is real. Saward is right when he states, "The objections to women's ordination are Christological." Christ the Bridegroom as a functional part of Christology is eliminated by women's ordination. The arguments against women's ordination are thus on sound traditional theological ground, because such a traditional Christology is incompatible with an inclusive practice in regard to the leadership of women.

Yet it cannot be denied that nuptial imagery for divine/human relations is a foundational biblical concept. Rethinking the hierarchical ordering of male and female relations and the heterosexist implications of an exclusively male/female model forces us to consider rethinking the hierarchical ordering of divine/human relations. Nuptial imagery does not necessitate a top-down style, but instead speaks to the sacramental quality Christians attribute to the mystery of two becoming one. In an inclusive Christology we will need to consider what it means to say Christ and the church become one flesh. This will perhaps lead to a consideration of the possibilities for real communal action on the part of a church that sees itself as having integrity and as being capable of agency.

Priest and King

In addition to the designation of Christ as Bridegroom of the church, two other designations that have had broad usage in the church are those of Christ as High Priest and as King. The reference to Christ as Bridegroom, however, is more a description of the nature of Christ, while the titles of Priest and King are really a statement about Christ's work in redemption, how Christ performs the act of salvation. Seeing Christ as High Priest and as King has resulted in some very exclusive practices in the church, and continues to have negative consequences.

The monastic period of 900 to 1100 C.E. has been called uncompromisingly Christocentric. Yet this intense focus on the Christ did not involve, with minor heretical exceptions, an investigation into the nature of Christ, as had the councils. Instead, reflection during this period was mostly on the plan of salvation.

Salvation through Christ presented a problem for theologians, firstly, because God had to undergo death, something of which the divine nature is in itself incapable. And second, once that had been worked out, it was still a problem that God would demand a victim for the divine wrath, a view that had the consequence of picturing God as bloodthirsty and vengeful.

The solution of the first problem lay in a distinction between the proper work of God, which is salvation, and what Peter Damian called the "alien work" of God, which would be to suffer and die. Frequently a text in Isaiah (28:21) was used to support this idea. In fact, most of the interpretation of the salvific work of Christ in his sacrifice on the cross comes from "typological" interpretation of the Old Testament, in which texts of the Hebrew Bible were interpreted as explicitly prefiguring the events recorded in the New Testament.

As sacrifice, Christ fulfilled what had been perceived only dimly in the sacrifices of the Jews. The "perfect" sacrifice of Christ also made it possible for Christians to ignore the ceremonial laws of the Hebrew Bible and not feel bound by them, "for whatever was carried out typologically in those sacrifices is completely fulfilled in the immolation of the Lamb that takes away the sins of the world."[12] In such typological interpretation, the sacrifice of Isaac was particularly meaningful. Abraham symbolized God, a Father who was willing to sacrifice his only son.

Another type of the sacrifice, and a crucial one, was the high priest Melchizedek, who "brought out bread and wine; he was priest of God Most High [Gen. 14:18]." Since the earliest times of the church, this text in Genesis had been read as a prefiguration of the eucharist and was thus a vehicle for the identification of Christ as the one true High Priest. In coming to view the atoning or reconciling work of Christ as a sacrifice, the eucharist became increasingly important. Anselm stated, "Just as there is one Christ who sacrificed himself for us, so there is one offering and one sacrifice that we offer in the bread and wine."[13] Christ thus became both priest and victim at the same time, and the paradox of a dying God could be resolved. God as victim is also God as celebrant. The suffering and death of the "God-man" leads to redemption and can thus be a "proper work" of God.

But while this interpretation of Christ as both priest and victim helps one part of the problem of redemption, it does not answer the question of *why* God wanted a sacrifice at all. Here again it was the brilliant Benedictine and exiled archbishop of Canterbury, Anselm, who provided a way out. Anselm formulated a complex idea of "rightness," a word that for him meant the truth or the true and real order of things. This did not only apply to persons; there was a rightness to the universe, a moral order of things, which had been upset by "Adam's" first sin. This upset could only be set right by the "right," or "true" if you will, action of another human being, the New Adam. Thus, God did not require the sacrifice of Jesus on the cross to satisfy the anger of God at humanity. Instead, it was necessary that the very order of the universe, which God was, in a sense, sworn to uphold, be restored to truth and justice by a perfect sacrifice.[14]

In the death and resurrection of Christ the "true order" of things is restored, in a historical sense. The primary focus of God's work in Christ is human history. Under the guidance of Christ the whole of human history, all times and events, are redirected toward the salvation of humanity. This immense historical achievement was laid out most explicitly in the work of Bernard of Clairvaux. He called Christ "King of all ages."[15] King was, of course, a title for God as well, but during this "uncompromisingly Christocentric" period, it became a title for Christ. Thus, in addition to a priestly role for Christ, in which he is connected to the Levitical priesthood, he also now has a royal role, in which he is also connected to the royal line of David. Christ becomes completely sovereign over history, the "Lord of History."

Christ becomes, therefore, both Priest and King, titles that have remained attached to his work in salvation throughout the history of the church. The consequences of these views are obviously enormous, but we will consider only a few that bear on our theme.

Christ as High Priest has his sacrificial ministry carried out by a visible priest in this theology. All the forms of the priesthood derive their authority from "his" sacerdotal office. It is not necessary to repeat again all the arguments against the ordination of women, but simply to underline the explicit connection between the designation of Christ as High Priest and the necessity for an exclusively male priesthood.

> Now it is precisely as a person with a particular gender that a priest, with the grace of the sacrament, images Christ, is his efficacious sign. S. Thomas tells us that "sacramental signs represent what they signify by a natural resemblance," in other words, to be a sacramental sign of Christ the High Priest a Christian priest must at least *look like* Christ in his human appearance, obviously not with regard to secondary characteristics (hair color and length, height, age, about none of which we can be absolutely certain) but to that which we do know—Christ's humanity in its particular gender, his maleness.[16]

The designation of Christ as a High Priest in the line of Melchizedek perpetuates the idea of the priesthood as an exclusive clique, to which not everyone can be admitted. The result seems less to have been the elevation of Christ, as was the explicit intention, but to elevate one group of humans to the status of co-redeemers.

But there is a deeper and still more problematic difficulty with the designation of Christ as both victim and priest. While Anselm may have neatly provided a

Platonic solution to the problem of why God needs a victim, for most Christians the penal theory of the atonement does not mean that God had to punish somebody. This is part of what many have labeled either the scapegoat mentality (Thomas Szaz, Henry Nicholson, and Eric Neumann) or the appropriate victim (Jean Baker Miller). Neumann also discusses scapegoat psychology from a Jungian perspective. For people in general, it is terribly difficult to acknowledge evil as one's own, because internal consciousness is not sufficiently developed to admit of such a potentially conflictual idea. So evil is experienced as something alien. Evil must be projected onto somebody so that it can be dealt with and destroyed. "It is our subliminal awareness that we are actually not good enough for the ideal values which have been set before us that results in the formation of the shadow,"[17] Eric Neumann says, recognizing that minorities and those marginal to society are ordinarily the scapegoats.

Women's role as scapegoat or appropriate victim has only recently been recognized. Miller points out the ways in which Christian mythology—Eve, for example—has perpetuated the idea of feminine evil, so that women are forced to accept "men's unsolved problems, the things they fear they will find if they open Pandora's box."[18]

In Christianity the values of the victim are idealized, particularly in the central idea of redeemer as victim. Sacrifice, passive acceptance of suffering, humility, meekness, all are held up to women as the model for Christian behavior.

The accompanying emphasis on the maleness of the one supreme Victim may appear paradoxical. If women are most appropriately victims, then they should be the perfect models of the ideal Victim. But the imposition of an impossible barrier to identification with the supreme Victim means that women are never given any credit for their sacrifices and are denied the dignity of an active role in the redemptive process. As Mary Daly has said, "Women, though encouraged to imitate the sacrificial love of Jesus, and thus willingly accept the victim's role, remain essentially identified with Eve and evil. Salvation comes only through the male."[19]

Christ as High Priest lends authority and credibility to an exclusive caste, the priesthood. Christ as Victim functions to shift responsibility for human wrongdoing onto a whipping boy, a shift that may have been a cause for Christianity to be co-opted so many times into scapegoating. What is the role of Christians in scapegoating the Jews (the murderers of Christ)? Black people (the sin of Cain)? Women (the temptress)? Must we always be finding somebody else to blame?

One last and particularly poignant example of the result of a Christology of Christ the Victim is recorded in Dell Martin's book *Battered Wives*. A woman writes of her life of abuse and answers the question often asked of abused women, "Why didn't you seek help?"

> I did. Early in our marriage I went to a clergyman, who, after a few visits, told me that my husband meant no real harm, that he was just confused and felt insecure. I was encouraged to be more tolerant and understanding. Most important, I was told to forgive him the beatings just as Christ had forgiven me from the cross. I did that, too."[20]

The centrality of Christ in the role of High Priest/ Victim in the redemptive process leads to his designation as King or Lord. He effects human salvation and thus comes to control history. A problem emerges with this additional designation, however, since if Christ controls history, what happens to free will?

It is clear in the theology of this Christocentric period that one of the results of a Christology of Christ's rulership is to imperil human choice. Gottschalk, following the Augustinian example, maintained that in the passage "God was in Christ, reconciling the world unto himself, not imputing their trespasses unto them [2 Cor. 5:19, KJV]," the term world only referred to the elect.[21] Augustine had talked of a "fixed number of the predestined."[22] The doctrine that some are preordained to be saved and others damned, it was maintained, does not require that God causes them to be damned. But Anselm rightly concluded that "if we assert free will in some, predestination disappears in them."

Although Christians have abandoned the doctrine of predestination, we have not questioned to any great extent the rulership of Christ over history. But again we must ask what agency is left to a Christian church whose destiny is sewed up already in the direction of human history by Christ? As in our search for an appropriate victim in Christ, are we not here again shirking responsibility for history and throwing it all onto Christ's shoulders? How can we possibly be judged for that for which we have no responsibility? This paradox of divine sovereignty and human responsibility is as old as thought, and its resolution is never easy. Christ the King, however, solves it to the exclusion of human responsibility.

If Christians do not accept responsibility for themselves in history as a church, they can easily be led along by whatever political power is in place by the view that this or that is "God's will." A church without a grasp of its historical responsibility is no fit covenant partner for the God who was willing to be one of us.

Liberal Jesus

A wholly different approach to Christology is that of liberalism. The "father" of liberal Christology, Friedrich Schleiermacher, starts his Christology not from an assumption of Jesus' divinity, but quite radically from his humanity. Jesus for Schleiermacher is the human being par excellence, the human being created as God intended it. Jesus was divine because he was fully conscious of God. This is how we can speak of his divinity.[23]

Thus, we can summarize the liberal approach to Christology as one of immanence. The discontinuities between the human and the divine are broken down, and instead a strong insistence emerges on the continuity between human beings and their Creator. Much is made of our "being in the image of God." God is more present in the creation, and far more available to us. Likewise, we have the possibility of being like God. In this latter vein, Jesus is not different from us in the kind of God-consciousness he exhibited, but only in the degree.

For liberals the work of this God-conscious Jesus has changed as well. In the work of Horace Bushnell, the "American Schleiermacher," this shift is most explicitly demonstrated. Joseph Bellamy, an expositor of the Calvinist Christology, wrote *True Religion Delineated.* In this work, the last hurrah of the older Calvinism in nineteenth-century American Protestant thought, Christ is shown as sacrificed to satisfy God's "honor." In a rather blunt version of the penal theory of the atonement, Bellamy shows that God sends Christ to satisfy divine wrath.[24] Bushnell contributed greatly to disposing of this penal view of the atoning work of Christ, and offered as a substitute his version of God's moral work in the sacrifice of Christ as outlined in his work *The Vicarious Sacrifice*. God's work in Christ becomes far more indirect, involving not a sacrifice for sins committed, but an example of self-giving love that will win over erring humanity by the influence of character or what Bushnell calls "moral power."[25]

It would seem at first glance that this approach in liberalism to the person and work of Christ would lend itself far more easily to an inclusive practice on the part of the church to those usually considered outcast. This is especially true with regard to women, since the work of Christ is frequently likened to the indirect influence women exercise in culture. Bushnell repeatedly likens the work of Christ to the compassion and self-sacrifice of mothers. Several times in *The Vicarious Sacrifice* Bushnell argues that the work of Christ in bearing all our sins, in pouring out his sympathies, "run down, all day, as it were, by the wretched multitudes crowding about him," should not strike us as foreign because we witness it every day in the love of mother for her child. The mother bears "all its [the child's] pains and sicknesses on her own feeling, and when it is wronged, is stung herself, by the wrong put upon it, more bitterly far than the child. She takes every chance of sacrifice for it as her own opportunity."[26]

While on the surface this comparison may appear to value women and their activity more than had previously been the case in traditional theology, a closer look reveals severe problems. In her tremendously insightful work *The Feminization of American Culture*, Ann Douglas has analyzed this trend toward "feminizing" Jesus on the part of nineteenth-century liberalism. Douglas rightly protests that this is not feminism in theology, but feminizing, the application of stereotypical attitudes about women to religion. The opposition of this approach to the older, male-dominated concepts in theology

> is incomplete and finally unimaginative; patriarchy is denied, but truly matriarchal values are not espoused. Strength, as essential to genuinely feminine as to genuinely masculine social and intellectual structures, is absent; weakness itself, no matter how unintentionally, is finally extolled.[27]

The liberal Jesus, here a sentimentalized Mom coddling her children into redemption, finally ends up excluding the Christ. In the name of overcoming dualism, the activity of God in Christ is finally denied.

There are good and sound social and political reasons for this type of Christology emerging in the nineteenth century. The values of Christianity that would challenge the competitiveness of rising capitalistic industrialization had to be controlled. Increasingly, religion found itself pushed to the private sphere in the society, where its function, like that of women, was to carry the values of cooperation and integration, but to carry them in ways that would not interfere with their denial in other spheres. Capitalism could not afford a God who was capable of actively judging injustices, and so, like women, God in Christ was deemed to work by moral suasion instead of direct action. In addition to reinforcing the exclusion of both women and Jesus from the mainstream of public life, this Christology continued to perpetuate exclusive practices as regards women within the church as well. Bushnell denied that women could be ministers precisely on the grounds of their Christlikeness.[28]

Another serious consequence of this liberal view of Jesus was tacitly to accept the limitation of the field of the work of his church. If Jesus was to persuade by example, certainly this meant that the church could do no other. The church was thereby confined in its activity to the private, unobtrusive, and fundamentally powerless role of not-too-active conscience for the nation. This is worth particularly close attention, since it is this Christology which continues to inform North American Protestantism.

Christologies of exclusion, which have operated by scapegoating some in or out of the church in favor of others, clearly cannot carry the metaphor of the Body of Christ. "Body" suggests an integral functioning of equals, which Christology must take into account.

INCLUSIVE CHRISTOLOGIES

The Androgynous Christ

There have been several attempts in the history of the church to correct the male domination of the redemptive process. While Aquinas was working out his famous synthesis of faith and reason, which resulted in the conclusion that Christ could only have been male, Julian of Norwich, a mystic anchorite, was having visions of Jesus' maternity.

Julian's major work was *Revelations of Divine Love*, a record of the seventeen "shewings" vouchsafed to her after a severe illness at the age of thirty. One cannot read the *Revelations* and not be struck by the Trinitarian emphasis. It is everywhere. "For," wrote Julian, "the Trinity is God, and God is Trinity. The Trinity is our Maker. The Trinity is our Keeper. The Trinity is our Lover." (See chapters 3 and 4.) It was shown to Julian that the three properties of the blessed Trinity are Fatherhood, Motherhood, and Lordship.

Our substance, an expression that seems to mean our soul, is a "higher part" and comes from God the Father; our "sensuality," in which we are "grounded and rooted," an expression for our physical nature, comes from God the Mother, who is also the second person of the Trinity or Christ. Thus Jesus Christ represents the property of motherhood: "I saw that the second Person, who is our Mother substantially—the same very dear Person is now become our Mother sensually."

It is appropriate that it is God the Mother or Christ who takes "our made kind." The work of Christ, "mother's service," is "nearest, readiest and surest; nearest, for it is most like us; readiest, for it is most of love; surest, for it is most of truth." "Christ feeds like a mother, but more than she, for he feeds with himself and gives us his breast, his sweet, open side."

The redemptive role of Christ is thus that of advocate within the Godhead itself, and guide for humanity. Christ is the one who cares for our needs and corrects our faults, but also the one to whom we run when distressed and afraid. Christ would "have us behave as the meek child, saying thus: 'My kind Mother, my gracious Mother, my most dear Mother, have mercy on me. I have made myself foul and unlike to thee; and I cannot or may not amend it but with thy help and grace." (See chapters 58–61.)

While her language is strikingly un-Thomist, Julian's work is not a direct challenge to Aquinas's hierarchy of being. Humans are both spirit and matter, and matter is always lower than spirit. Yet she differs from Aquinas in that matter as sensuality belongs to the Godhead as well as spirit, and is part of the Trinitarian nature.

Further, the work of Christ is guidance and nurture, not the satisfaction of order. Julian comes close to having Christ take on the characteristics of Mary in medieval piety, who became humanity's mediator and advocate because she was not only the Mother of God, but our mother as well.

A Christology that provides an even more explicit alternative to the male-centered ideas we have examined is that of "Mother" Ann Lee, founder of the Shakers, described in chapter 1. Ann Lee left no writings herself, being completely illiterate, but her followers recorded much of what she preached. A follower, Eunice Goodrich, reported:

> Samuel Fitch believed the gospel, being at Watervliet, and having received a great manifestation of light and understanding said to Mother Ann, "Christ is called the Second Adam, and thou art the Second Eve." She answered, "Flesh and blood has not revealed it unto thee, Samuel, but God has" [cf. Matt. 16:16-17].[29]

Ann Lee taught that since sin was "first planted" in a female, the overthrow of sin must come by way of a woman "and its final destruction must begin where its foundation was first laid, and from whence it first entered the human race."[30]

Almost a century after Ann Lee, Mary Baker Eddy offered the revelation of the Motherhood of God (as noted in chapter 1): "In divine science we have not as much authority for considering God masculine, as we have for considering Him feminine, for Love imparts the clearest idea of Deity."[31]

Such androgynous Christologies clearly press at the boundaries of existing theologies and show the inadequacy of an exclusively male pattern for redemption.

Further, the proponents of the androgynous Christ also provided a challenge to male leadership in the church and to the role of the church in the world.

Anchorism in the tumultuous fourteenth century may be seen as a form of social protest: a critique of things as they are, at any rate. Julian's claim to spiritual authority in her call to be an anchorite was most definitely upheld by the church. Women's leadership was encouraged in the communities of Ann Lee and Mary Baker Eddy; Ann Lee's ban on sexual activity was certainly liberating for women when safe and sure birth control was unknown. From their persecutions, it is clear that Shakerism and Christian Science were perceived by the larger culture as subversive of its order. Shakers were violently handled during the Revolutionary War for their pacifism.

But despite all these changes, the androgynous alternatives offered are ambivalent about the contribution of the female. In Julian's thought, the female is the lower matter that completes the male spirit. While "feminized," the process is still a hierarchy in which the male is more valuable than the female.

In nineteenth-century sectarian thought, change comes either by denying female sexuality or by trading on its stereotypic qualities as spiritually "purer." In either case, women's equality is purchased by denying their full humanity.

Androgyny does not seem to guarantee equality for women. Inclusion of women under the same paradigms of dominance and submission does not change the function of these Christologies.

Christ the Liberator

The theologians of liberation pose a christological alternative that attempts to change the paradigm. In both North and South America, theologians deeply concerned with the state of the church in the world have come to the conclusion that theology is the "second act." The "first act" is the commitment to social change in a world increasingly divided into large groups of oppressed peoples and small groups of oppressors.

Several works represent this trend. The beginning is found in Gustavo Gutiérrez's *A Theology of Liberation* (1971). Since 1971, Leonardo Boff, a Brazilian, has written *Jesus Christ Liberator* (1972); Jon Sobrino, a Salvadoran, *Christology at the Crossroads* (1976); and José Miranda, a Mexican, *Being and the Messiah* (1977). In North America, Rosemary Radford Ruether has recently completed *To Change the World: Christology and Cultural Criticism* (1981). Frederick Herzog's *Justice Church* (1980) focuses on Jesus and power.

As opposed to Christologies that deny human agency and creativity, these writers assert that the human being is a "co-participant in his own salvation."[32] Human temporal progress is understood as a genuine continuation of the work of creation. Human beings are not passive bodies manipulated by Christ the Head or Christ the Bridegroom, but freed by Christ to be agents of liberation.[33]

It is characteristic of Christologies of liberation that the beginning point is with the Jesus of history. There are striking differences between this beginning with Jesus of Nazareth and liberalism's focus on Jesus, however. The "relevance" of the historical Jesus to the contemporary situation is mediated by a social analysis of reality and a liberation hermeneutics that interprets the Christian tradition in light of this social analysis.

Boff explicitly insists on the relevance of the historical Jesus for liberation in the twentieth century because through tools of social analysis, specifically Marxist categories of the dialectics of history, he sees a "structural similarity between Jesus' day and our own." Jesus' time was also characterized by extremes of oppression and domination. Therefore, focus on the historical Jesus "puts us in direct contact with his liberative program and the practices with which he implements it."[34]

This appropriation of the dialectics of Marxist social analysis enables the theologians of liberation to avoid the errors of liberalism. While in contact with the Jesus of history, liberals adopted a functionalist approach to history, which stressed the idea of balance and harmony and analyzed society as an organic whole with complementary parts.[35] In examining the theology of Schleiermacher, Herzog points out that "Schleiermacher did not take note of the conflicts in society as he drew the analogy between church and civil government. Anyone who today takes over Schleiermacher's view also appropriates a harmonious view of society that has proved deceptive."[36] Thus liberal theology did not take account of the struggle that is at the heart of the historical task. This liberal theology, while seemingly radical in some of its premises, could coexist with conservative and even reactionary social ideologies.

Theologians of liberation, on the contrary, are concerned with the man Jesus, but moreover with his activity in history, which they see as paradigmatic. The liberal focus on the man Jesus, for example, was still exclusive of women because, after all, Jesus did not become a woman. For Rosemary Ruether, a liberation theologian, the fact of Jesus' becoming a man is crucially related to the type of man he became. Jesus Christ the liberator of the oppressed is one who sides with those on the bottom of the power structures of the world. In his time, women were certainly among the most powerless of the society. These last are therefore first in the kingdom. Furthermore, Jesus' way of being as a *male* is a judgment on the male way of being in the world as rulers who "lord it over" others (Matthew 20:25-27). Jesus' maleness, according to Ruether, is part of his criticism of patriarchy.[37] This conclusion demonstrates the way in which the concentration of theologians of liberation on power struggles helps to avoid the narrow individualism of liberalism's historical Jesus.

Theologians of liberation, particularly in Latin America, are concerned with the eschatological meaning of Christ. In the historically perilous situation in which they find themselves, it is important not to allow the Christ who identifies with the oppressed to succumb to Christ the Victim. Gutiérrez relies on the promise made to Abraham that is "fulfilled in Christ, the Lord of history and of the cosmos. In him, we are 'the "issue"' of Abraham, and so heirs by promise. (Gal. 3:29) This is the mystery which remained hidden until the fullness of time."[38]

The need to claim the promise unfortunately leads Gutiérrez into a denial of the Jewish right to the promise. Jesus is the "mystery the Jews don't understand."

> When the infidelities of the Jewish people rendered the Old Covenant invalid, the Promise was incarnated both in the proclamation of a New Covenant, which was awaited and sustained by the "remnant," as well as in the promises which prepared and accompanied its advent.[39]

According to him, the sins of Israel have rendered it unacceptable, and the guarantees given to the Jews by God are no longer valid.[40]

The promise dominates the writings of the Latin American theologians of liberation, and they talk of the presence and future of Christ in triumphalist terms. Christ "himself is present and lives a way of life that has already surpassed the limitations of a world of death and realized every dimension of all its possibilities."[41] All history comes under the control of this event; a "total cosmic-human-divine realization of fullness" occurred in Christ. All things in an "ascending dynamics of reality" converge in Christ.[42]

Another example of this type of Christ-dominance is the striking Messiah Jesus language that Herzog employs. In consistently referring to Jesus as Messiah Jesus in *Justice Church*, Herzog states that his intention is to recognize the Jewish origins of Christianity. It is true that a focus on the Jewishness of Jesus does emphasize our primary identity as Christians with the history of Judaism and with Jewish thought. It is questionable, however, whether the term Messiah Jesus accomplishes this. Herzog states that he seeks dialogue between Jews and Christians. But the way into dialogue is not to preempt the entire basis of the discussion and to define things, as usual, the Christian way. Jesus is *not* Messiah for the Jews.

Rosemary Ruether is one theologian of liberation who has been especially sensitive to issues of anti-Semitism. Ruether understands that "the anti-Judaic patterns of Christian theology were and are still today tied to a dogma of fulfilled messianism."[43] The christological basis necessitates the repudiation of the Jewish expectation of a Messiah who is not Jesus of Nazareth. Christology must give up this realized messianism and talk of the Christ in terms "which are proleptic and anticipatory, rather than final and fulfilled."[44] We must also come to see the limits of Christology in its contextualization in the life of a particular people who are living out one stream of history. As humans, we do not like unresolved contradictions in our theology, but an open-ended approach to Christology appears the only way to excise anti-Semitism from Christology.

The finality of Christian theology remains a problem in Christologies of liberation. Gutiérrez talks of a "Christo-finalized history," a phrase that appears to fly in the face of his equally strong emphasis on human freedom and agency. The importance of human co-participation with God in history is eroded by this absolute control left to God in Christ. Further, Christ as the King of history co-opts non-Christian peoples for the Christian task. The cosmic Christ rules over all.

Christologies of liberation are certainly more open to those formerly excluded from the central themes of theology: women, persons of color, and the poor. And it may be that the Latin American situation demands such a two-edged Christology in order to sustain Christian life. But it must be stressed that this is a Christology for that context, and limits become apparent apart from that context.

THE RELATIONAL CHRIST

A Christology more appropriate to the North American situation is that recently proposed by Tom Driver (*Christ in a Changing World*) and Carter Heyward (*The Redemption of God*). These approaches are labeled "relational" because both theologians begin with the Buberian "I and Thou."

> Life and relationship are synonymous. Everything
> that lives interacts with its environment, and even
> the individual organism, considered in itself, is a
> community of cells and organs, the whole giving
> meaning, form and purpose to each of its mem-
> bers.[45]

This theological premise appears to me to address
the North American situation, because we are enmeshed in a divide-and-conquer mentality in which
the churches are played off against one another in denominationalism, in which scapegoating for our problems is a national pastime, in which racism, sexism,
and anti-Semitism, all on the rise, have created a
scenario in a "war of all against all." Several commen-
tators on the national scene have noted the current un-
employment scene and the difference in national reac-
tion to the 1930s. In the 1930s, one observer noted,
Americans had a sense of all being in the same boat.
Currently, Americans are divided among themselves.

This is particularly true in relation to the interlock-
ing problems of racism and sexism. Ordinarily treated
as separate when considered at all, these two patterns
of American society assume a stratification in which
white women and black men are played off against
each other and denied entry into the white male club of
power and access to power.[46] Affirmative action positions demonstrate this dynamic very well. A new position is advertised for a woman or minority person. The
job applicants are therefore competing against one
another for an economic crumb, while the question is
never raised as to why only one position is available.
This competition is intolerable for women of color,
who are torn as to where their minority loyalties lie.[47]

Theology in North America needs a paradigm shift,
in Driver's term. We Christians need to re-envisage our

situation theologically and find new responses to our problems. The paradigm shift that both Driver and Heyward propose is twofold. The first fundamental shift comes from the realization that history is no longer fixed and immutable to the modern consciousness. Everything that makes sense to us does so because it is part of a relational field of meaning. In this relational matrix, absolute claims about God and Christ empty them of meaning. Says Driver, "We are in danger of losing Christ utterly through our attempts to make Him a fixed and eternal point for all time."

The second paradigm shift is the recognition of the absolutely essential relation between theology and ethics. This shift becomes possible when theology is a reflection on shared praxis. Heyward observes, "The theologian's on-going constructive task is to discern common assumptions which are emerging in the praxis out of which and to which she speaks."[48] From this theological premise, it is clear that what we say and what we do are inseparable. We begin where the church is and struggle to discern our responsibility in history, to figure out "What next?"[49]

Both Driver and Heyward insist on human responsibility for the "What next?" and have discerned that theologies which have proposed waiting on God for the next move have led to human irresponsibility in history and to the moral failures of Christians in dealing with situations like Auschwitz and Cambodia. The decisive step is away from a sole reliance on God's responsibility for establishing justice, toward humanity's power in relation to effect the good, to effect justice in this place and at this time. This is their unequivocal answer to Heyward's question, "To what extent are we responsible for our own liberation in history?"

The decision to pursue a Christology within the context of ethics necessitates methodological changes. For Heyward this is the hermeneutical norm of love of neighbor.[50] This is not love of neighbor for the sake of God, but the way of being in relation with another in which God's creative power, that which effects justice—right relation—in history is incarnated.

For Driver, to pose a Christology in the context of ethics means giving up certain presuppositions about Jesus. It means refusing to let the Christian conscience hide behind Jesus in asking "What would Jesus do?" It means freeing ourselves from the tyranny of tradition that renders irrelevant problems which have not been seen in the past, or which appear in another guise today. Most emphatically, it requires understanding existence as relationship. Most crucially, it means giving up such terms as the only begotten Son, King, High Priest, and Messiah of Israel. These all connote the "one and only." These terms all focus on the once-for-all uniqueness of Christ. In consequence, "they obscure the vital point that the reality of Christ is a relation of mutual dependence, an I-Thou relation."[51]

This insight is the primary reason this Christology of Relation is posed as a Christology for the Body. A Christology for the Body brings about the praxis of inclusiveness within the church. Christologies of King, of High Priest, of Victim, of the Liberal Jesus have all been shown to end up excluding vast numbers of people and promoting an elitism in which some members consider themselves to be higher than others.

A Christology of Relation, on the contrary, is one in which the very being of Christ comes about through the relation of the members to one another. Dorothee Soelle expresses this exquisitely in a poem quoted by Heyward.

and what
> will David do without Jonathan
> and Karl Marx without Engels
> and Mary without Elizabeth
> and Ché Guevara without Fidel
> and Jesus without John
> and Dietrich without Eberhard?

"And what," continues Heyward, "will I do without you?"[52]

A Christology of Relation means giving up Christocentrism, what Dorothee Soelle has called Christofascism. The centrality of Christ to history came about as a result of the delay of the Kingdom. Consequently, as was pointed out earlier, Christ was asserted to have already come, in some sense, in final form. This shifted attention from the future to the past. The church came to regard itself as the Kingdom of God, "flawed in fact, but perfect in principle."[53]

Driver is concerned with persons who have been rendered "weak, invisible or ashamed by the Church's affirmation of Jesus Christ as the Center of all things." These folk include:

> 1. Those who are not male, as is Christ, the center of all things.
> 2. Those who are neither white nor Semitic, as is Christ, the center of all things.
> 3. Those who are born without inheritance, unlike Christ, the center of all things.
> 4. Those who feel strongly their sexuality, unlike Christ, the center of all things.
> 5. Those who have never known, and do not wish to know, Abraham as their father, who have other fathers and mothers to honor, unlike Christ, the center of all things. . . .[54]

The centrality of Christ cuts the nerve of ethical effort in other ways. As Driver points out, "One may follow a leader, but not a center."[55] The church with Christ as its center is unlikely to follow Christ out of its own little enclave and into the world.

The centrality of Christ is related to Christ's once-for-all character as traditionally conceived. Christ as once-for-all stops history. Nothing new can ever creep into our Christology. If Christ is the one and only center of history, now and forevermore, then Christianity is God's last and definitive word to humanity. A certain cultural imperialism is visible here, which denies to all non-Christian peoples the ultimate validity of their religious traditions.

The imperial Christ threatens human freedom and undermines human responsibility. The consequences of this are becoming only too apparent to us as we race with ourselves to stop the nuclear arms race before it stops us. An exponent of the imperial Christ, Billy Graham, nevertheless has come out strongly in his later career for disarmament. This is a decisive shift from his earlier posture as apostle of the cold war. But still Graham reminds his audiences that there "will only be peace when the Messiah comes" and talks about nuclear war as the scenario for the Second Coming of Jesus, with humanity saved from its destructive impulses only by God's intervention: "Until the flaw in our human nature is corrected, we will continue to stand at the edge of Armageddon. . . . We do not have the capacity to control our technology. We do not have the strength as the human race to save the planet without God's help."[56] The motive to act and act now is undermined by Graham's reliance on a Messiah to do it all for us. The capacity of human beings to stop their own destructiveness is impugned and hence weakened.

But a Christology of Relation insists emphatically that we are all, and this includes God, in this together. God has chosen to give human beings responsibility for history, and it is our fault if we do not take it. Likewise, it is to our credit if we do. As Heyward points out, "To my knowledge, there is no Christian theologian who has held unequivocally that, just as evil is the result of humanity's wrong choices, so too, good is the result of humanity's right choices."[57]

The pattern for this relational theology is one in which we are caught up with God in the process of redemption, in which humanity is free to be responsible for history and to be in relation to God and to one another. There are some sound theological precedents for this perspective. Trinitarian thinking about the nature of God means thinking about the eternal as existing in relation, in which there is no subordination or inequality. Jürgen Moltmann, in his work *The Trinity and the Kingdom*, states that he has come to believe that the economic trinity (the activities of God in the world) and the immanent Trinity (the Trinity considered apart from God's saving activities in the world) cannot be considered separately. In fact, the relatedness of the Trinity considered as immanent cannot be understood apart from the relationship of the triune God to the world, also a relationship of mutuality.

Trinitarian thinking that brings together the characteristics of the immanent and economic Trinity means connecting the equality and mutuality of the persons of the Trinity to the actions of God in the world: creation, redemption, and sanctification. Human response to

God's creative, redemptive, and sanctifying activity in the world should be characterized by relatedness in unity and co-equality.

It may be thought that the price of an inclusive Christology is too high—that it entails giving up Christ. To some extent this is true, if Christ is conceived so exclusively that Jews, women, and the poor are systematically kept from identifying with "him."

But an inclusive Christology that points away from Christ and toward human life in responsible action can be truly liberating. It can liberate Christians to stop scapegoating Jews, women, and blacks, and to take responsibility for our history. Christ is no longer seen as patiently standing by, waiting for "his" children to come running when they fall. Both the failures *and* the successes are most definitely our responsibility.

This is not to say that God is not with us. But to be with someone is to take one's place alongside them, helping but not controlling. The Body of Christ metaphor is enfleshed by a relational Christology that opens us to recognize the ways in which human connectedness brings God into the world.

We have already articulated the presence and future of God with us in different language than we use for the time God was with us in Jesus whom we call the Christ. God is present with us in the Spirit.

The Holy Spirit is the most neglected member of the Trinity, and for good cause, as we shall see. It is to the Spirit that we turn to sustain us when we take hold of the reins of our history.

Chapter 4 THE SPIRIT OF JUSTICE

JUST AS the metaphor of the Body of Christ has been subverted by Christologies that divide the body and exclude some in favor of others, so too the metaphor of the Poor has been undermined. A feminized pneumatology (that is, a doctrine of the Holy Spirit) has given the church the "poor in spirit," where spirituality is conceived as otherworldly and largely passive. Such a Spirit is effectively restrained from challenging the church to act in solidarity with the poor. It is necessary to claim the relational qualities assigned to a feminized Spirit, but also to free the Spirit from a narrowed, delimited sphere of the stereotypically feminine role of persuader.

The Holy Spirit has been feminized in the sense that the action of the Spirit is characterized in stereotypically feminine ways. As Jean Baker Miller has observed, the qualities associated with the feminine are cooperation, integration, and affiliation. But likewise these qualities are undervalued and attached to the negative qualities of vulnerability, weakness, helplessness, and dependency.

If the Spirit is theologically the most neglected member of the Trinity, a case can be made for its neglect precisely because the action of the Spirit is understood to have these same qualities of indirection as the feminine.

Certain theologians have directly associated the Spirit with the feminine. Paul Tillich raised the problem he saw in a Protestantism deprived even of Marian imagery of "a one-sided male determined symbolism" and proposed the action of the Spirit, "the motherquality of giving birth, carrying, and embracing, and at the same time, of calling back, resisting independence of the created and swallowing it," as a corrective.[1]

Yet, even when the connection to the feminine is not explicit, the action of the Spirit has come to be regarded, especially in contemporary Protestantism but also in Catholic Pentecostalism, as a quality of dependence on God in the life of the individual believer and of cohesiveness in the community of believers. But this is only one aspect of the action of the Spirit, itself hampered because of undervaluation by contemporary culture. The Spirit is thus confined to one set of activities, viewed in feminized terms and limited in scope.

The history of the doctrine of the Holy Spirit is enormously complex and beyond the range of this study. But broad outlines can be sketched that reveal the origins of some of these difficulties. As Christologies of exclusion have divided the church, pneumatologies of subordination and passivity have subverted its ability to act for justice in the world.

PNEUMATOLOGIES OF SUBORDINATION AND PASSIVITY

THE Holy Spirit in Christian thought is considered one of the three persons of the Trinity. Therefore, an examination of the problems in a doctrine of the Holy Spirit begins with Trinitarian theology.

Trinitarianism as a way of conceiving the biblical divine self-revelation is, however, a response primarily to attacks on the divinity of Christ. Thus even problems with the Holy Spirit have to be approached indirectly, a fact entirely symptomatic of the difficulties inherent in a doctrine of the Holy Spirit. The only real advantage is that Trinitarian theology itself is an attempt to do theology as the second act. The first act is the experience of God in Christ and of the power of God's reconciling activity in the post-Pentecostal church: "No one can say 'Jesus is Sovereign!' except by the Holy Spirit [1 Cor. 12:3]." The concept of the Trinity is an attempt to explain the experience believers have had of God's activity in the world.

This means, however, that the concept of the Trinity finds its origin in the incarnation. It is especially important, therefore, given the christological caveats raised in the preceeding chapter, to keep in mind that in no sense does a relational Christology mean a unitarian view of God. Unitarianism in theology is a strict monotheism, the view that there is one God and that while Jesus of Nazareth revealed much about God, he was himself in no sense God.

Relational Christology need not abolish the central tenet of the Christian faith that God was in Jesus. In the overall schema of this work, the relational Christology is an attempt to state what kind of God Jesus was and is.

If Jesus had been only a good man, even God's foremost prophet, his life would still be inspiring. But there would be no Holy Spirit and no need for a Trinity. The Trinity is ultimately the expression that God became incarnate in Jesus *and* that this presence of God in the world can still be directly experienced in the Holy Spirit.

Ironically, the history of the doctrine of the Holy Spirit in the Western Church reveals instead that attempts to secure the divinity of the human Jesus weakened the place of the Spirit and resulted at best in a duality, if not in outright monotheism.

The Soul of the Church

In the early and middle ages of the church the doctrine of the Holy Spirit emerged as a response to heresies that attempted to subordinate Christ and hence the Spirit to God (subordinationism or Arianism), or which attempted to reduce Christ and the Spirit to modes or manifestations of the one Supreme God (modalism or Sabellianism). Both of these controversies were christological in origin, but they had important consequences for the Spirit. As the church affirmed the divinity and consubstantiality of Christ, it encountered the necessity to define the Spirit as well. Was the Spirit a created angel or the Spirit of God?

The Nicene Creed in 325 had recognized the Spirit: "And we believe in the Holy Spirit." The Nicene-Constantinopolitan Creed, sixty-six years later, defined the Spirit as "the Lord and Giver of Life, who proceeds from the Father, who together with the Father and Son is adored and glorified, who spoke through the prophets." Thus by the late fourth century the Trinitarian position that the Holy Spirit is a person of the Godhead was established.

Unfortunately, these creedal affirmations did not remove the threat of the subordinationist and modalist controversies. The threat has remained and is present in more modern times in variants of modern liberalism. Schleiermacher was both subordinationist in his articulation of Christ as the firstborn of many and modalist in his view that the Trinity does not represent God as God is in true being—that there is, so to speak, an essential being of God that is behind the Trinity.[2]

There is a monarchy evident in this point of view that makes God, as supreme "Father," superior to the "Son" and the Spirit, a logical consequence of abandoning the Trinity. Furthermore, monotheistic monarchianism goes hand in hand with a political ideology of oppression.[3] As Jürgen Moltmann points out,

> The fundamental notion behind the universal is uniform religion: One God—one Logos—one humanity; and in the Roman Empire it was bound to be seen as a persuasive solution for any problems of a multi-national and multi-religious society. The universal ruler in Rome had only to be the image and correspondence of the universal ruler in heaven.[4]

This is ultimately the religion of patriarchy, which decrees the supreme rulership of one Father over all and from whom other authorities take their cue. Hierarchy introduces hierarchy: God the Father, father priest, father of the country, father in the family, and so on.

But this is precisely what the church *repudiated* in its first four centuries when it established the doctrine of the co-eternality and co-equality of the three members of the Trinity. Or did it?

The personhood of the Spirit was only the first stage in the development of a doctrine of the Holy Spirit. The second stage was the question of origin. While it seems an impossibly dry scholastic question to ask whether the Spirit proceeds from the "Father" alone, or from the "Father" and the "Son," it is a meaningful question in relation to its consequences.

The Nicene-Constantinopolitan Creed had stated that the Spirit proceeds from the "Father." In the West, via the thought of Augustine, who stressed the divine unity (Trin. 5, 9), a "double process," the phrase "and the Son" (filioque), was added to that creed. This addition was a substantial factor in the separation of the Eastern and Western Churches.[5]

Whatever these problems were in context,[6] for the Western Church the addition of the idea that the Holy Spirit proceeds both from the "Father" and from the "Son" caused both a subordination of the Spirit to the "first" two members of the Trinity, and a Christocentric bias.[7] The advantages of Trinitarian thought were curtailed and a tendency to view God as a solitary monarch was strengthened, along with a resultant support for patriarchy in society.

Other developments in the doctrine of the Holy Spirit aided this. A response to the modalists, and indeed to the numerous heretical challenges of the first four centuries, was the assertion that prophecy had ceased outside the institutional church. The Western Church found its assurance of the work of the Spirit in the threefold apostolic authority of canon, creed, and ecclesiastical office. This insistence on a Christocentric criterion for piety was in opposition to the East, where a more direct line was assumed between the movement of the Spirit and the "Father," and hence a more direct, mystical relationship between the soul and God was deemed possible. In the West, the pope as the Vicar of Christ controlled the access route to God via Christ via the Roman Church as the conduit of the Holy Spirit. Thus, as Tillich has noted, "the Roman Church became less flexible and more legalistic than the Eastern Churches. In Rome the freedom of the Spirit is limited by canon law. The Spiritual Presence is legally circumscribed."[8] The Spirit was subordinated to the other two members of the Trinity and identified with the visible, institutional church. The prophetic possibilities a more independent Spirit has for critique and challenge of the church were lost, since the Holy Spirit was effectively identified with the church as its soul.

The Sanctifier

It may at first appear curious that while the Reformation was based on the independence of the Spirit from the institutions of the Roman Church, the Reformers did not reopen conversations with the Orthodox Church. But a closer examination reveals that the Lutherans and Calvinists did not differ from their Augustinian model in regard to their fundamental assumptions about the role of the Spirit in relation to God the "Father" and God the "Son," and so held on to the *filioque*, thus leaving themselves open for the patriarchal tendencies of a resultant focus on God the Father.

The reformers repudiated the visible Spirit manifest as the soul of the church in favor of an invisible Spirit written on the heart, the Sanctifier. Luther did criticize the tendency to enthusiasm he saw in his colleague Karlstadt, who had "swallowed the Holy Ghost, feathers and all," and therefore attempted to secure some independence for the Holy Spirit in the external means of word and sacrament. But his doctrine of the church was not strong enough to bring it off.

The mainline reformers (Luther, Calvin, Zwingli) understood the Spirit as crucial to carrying out Christ's saving work, and this gave them the authority to challenge the Roman Church. They therefore abolished the concept of that church as the only saving institution. The church in Protestantism is a collection of believers *each* sanctified by the Spirit. Thus the sacraments of this church are secondary to the interior life in the Spirit of each individual believer. The tendency to "enthusiasm" prevails.

It may be argued that the reformers, particularly Calvin, did make the Holy Scriptures a visible Spirit. In Calvin's view, the biblical writers are passive "amanuenses of the Holy Spirit"[9] and the scriptures are the true voice of God. But the inner testimony of the sanctifying Spirit is necessary for Christians to believe in this book, and so an interiority remains. The tendency in the century that followed the Reformation was similar to that exhibited by the early church in dealing with heresies. Heresy is excluded by a detailed and legalistic presentation of orthodoxy. In the Roman Church, the authority resided in a visible institution; in the Protestant Church, in a book. In Protestant scholasticism's insistence on a supernatural book, inspired, infallible, and perfect, the Holy Spirit was relegated to the background. Likewise, the order of salvation was detailed. The emphasis fell on soteriology with little mention of the living Spirit.

In commenting unfavorably on this increased Protestant scholasticism in the seventeenth century, Bernard Holm, a Lutheran scholar, nevertheless applauds this approach to salvation. "Yet this Protestant *ordo salutis* was far sounder than the medieval approach; at least it was clearly seen that salvation involves 'passive' changes, i.e., that it is God's work alone. Here one finds unmistakable affirmation of Christ, of grace alone and not of works." Then he asks, "But why so little positive, explicit stress on the Spirit?"[10] There is so little stress on the Spirit because Christology has overtaken any doctrine of the Holy Spirit as a person of the Trinity and replaced it with an impersonal, controlling grace. The result is quite rightly a passivity of the believer.

With the Reformation and the Enlightenment, theology turned, or was forced, away from concern with God as substance toward God as subject. Reality was no longer seen as a divinely ordered cosmos surrounding and containing human beings. Humanity discovered its own subjectivity and with it discovered its ego. The center of the world became the perceiving human subject.

The two developments of Pietism and rationalism in Protestant theology in the eighteenth century reflect this shift to modernity. Paul Tillich has pointed out the similarity among Quakers, pietists, and rationalists. They all "looked within" the human subject for ultimate guidance and the assurance of truth. The Quakers had inner light; the pietists had the inner testimony of the Holy Spirit; the rationalists had the innate power of reason by which they could investigate and illuminate the secrets of nature, improve human society, and attain unending progress.[11]

The theology of John Wesley, also a product of this period, indicates an effort within Pietism to break out of this wholesale inwardness and to launch a new synthesis of inner experience and external holiness. God intends the creation of a holy people, and for Wesley this had to be an actual, visible, and experienced reality in the social as well as in the individual realm. Wesley thus sought a way beyond Pietism.

According to José Míguez Bonino, Wesley's attempt failed because his understanding of the human subject remained "incurably individualistic." Thus Wesley was unable to break out of the "straightjacket" of "the inherited theological framework of the *ordo salutis*." The individual had to go through a moralizing process that remained fundamentally at variance with his or her earthly, social, bodily life. The dualism, as Míguez Bonino terms it, means that "sanctification becomes the operation of a moral and spiritual self through the mediation of a divine moral code."[12]

It is this ideal, bourgeois self, the personality, which emerges at this point in Protestantism. The result for a doctrine of the Holy Spirit is most glaringly apparent in the theology of Friedrich Schleiermacher. Theology loses all objective grounding in Schleiermacher and is based on the feeling of ultimate dependence on God that the self experiences. This is not an emotional or enthusiastic response, but an "immediate self-consciousness." Such personal awareness as the basis of authority results in a psychologizing of the faith.

The Holy Spirit in Schleiermacher's schema becomes a common Spirit of religious trust in Jesus Christ that believers have with one another—it is a bond among the faithful. The Spirit as a person of the Trinity is decisively dissolved. A duality results, since the Holy Spirit is no longer the third person of the Trinity, but the divine power and the continuing presence of Christ.[13]

This is an ultimate failure of Trinitarian theology in

Protestantism, leading to a subordination of the Spirit in a kind of Christ-centered monotheism that reinforces monarchical patriarchalism. Here, however, the direction of theological reflection is reversed. Unlike the older orthodoxy, where the revelation of God's supreme "Fatherhood" legitimates human fatherhood, in liberalism it is the patriarchalism of the bourgeois culture of personality that legitimates *divine* fatherhood.

The neoorthodoxy of Karl Barth in the twentieth century was an attempt to reverse this direction of revelation once more and begin from God and not from human subjectivity. But this is nonetheless modern theology. Barth's God is Absolute Subject, not absolute substance. He states, "God's Word is God in his revelation. God reveals himself as Lord. He alone is the revealer. He is wholly revelation."[14] This is the revelation of one who is absolutely other to humanity—in Barth's view, the only possible answer to Schleiermacher. God's revelation is the "revelation of his rule . . . *over against* men, *in* men, *over* men, *for* men."[15] God's sovereignty is supremely God's subjectivity, the divine personality.

There is no real room at the top, so to speak, for a Trinity. The divine "I-ness" is taken up by the Almighty, and what remains is a revelation of this one subject in three modes. In God there is one self-consciousness that repeats itself three times.[16] The Holy Spirit loses all subjectivity apart from the sovereign God and becomes "the power that joins the Father and the Son."[17] The Spirit is reduced to relationship. In Schleiermacher's thought this relationship was interhuman; in Barth's thinking it is interdivine. The result is still a duality in which the Spirit is eliminated and the "Son" is barely distinguishable from the

"Father." This sovereignty is so complete that human freedom disappears and the human subject becomes wholly passive in the process of sanctification.

Doctrines of the Holy Spirit have alternated between tying the Spirit to a visible institution, the church, and relegating the Spirit to the interior life of the believer. The consequence in either case has been to undervalue the Spirit and to circumscribe the action of the Spirit, effectively restraining our appreciation for interhuman bonding and for the public, prophetic acts of the Spirit.

INDEPENDENT AND POLITICAL PNEUMATOLOGIES

A first step in restating a doctrine of the Holy Spirit in Trinitarian terms is a recognition of the social, political, and psychological implications of the subordination and passivity of the Spirit monotheistic theology has given us.

God the monarch, supremely free and sovereign over "his" creation, is a conception of domination. Only God is free under this rubric, and the people are "his" property. In traditional orthodoxy, God's absolute sovereignty and freedom mean domination, power, and possession. Liberalism in theology does not fundamentally provide an alternative to this schema, since the idea of sovereignty remains and is merely transferred to a human few.

Schleiermacherian liberalism deserves special attention at this point because it is a theological perspective returning to vogue in North American Protestantism and in American Catholic liberalism (David Tracy in North America and Leonardo Boff in Latin America) since the waning of Barthian neoorthodoxy after 1960. One observer even questions whether the new evangelicalism is

> really something new *within* evangelicalism, or is "it" the shaky, searching first steps of a reborn liberalism? . . . I wonder if history were not repeating itself rather than doing something new; perhaps paralleling the well-known changes in rhetoric and style that evangelical churches like the Methodist underwent several generations ago as their constituencies moved up the education and affluence ladders.[18]

Protestant liberalism seems once again to be affirmed, as Dean William Ferm writes in *The Christian Century*. Ferm claims a move beyond Schleiermacher's "inward experience of Christian people," which he finds "more narrow and specific than one that today's liberals would espouse." Today's liberal, asserts Ferm, includes under the heading of experience "one's total life, past and present, personal and social, aesthetic and scientific, mystical and moral."[19]

Ferm's own work demonstrates how this is still the inwardness of a few whose experience is elevated over the many and which becomes a vehicle of oppression. In his volume *Contemporary American Theologies: A Critical Survey* (1981), Ferm sets as his task an examination of black, feminist, and liberation theologians, among others, from the perspective that their particularist foci have resulted in "fractured faith," i.e., splintered versions of theology. Ferm asserts "the fundamental unity of all existence and experience."

But existence and experience are not unified for all people. That is exactly what blacks, women, and third-world people are saying: "Our experience is not your experience."[20] While certainly one must applaud Ferm's attempt to find a theological perspective that will unite and not divide, this cannot be achieved by elevating a theoretical unity of experience that does not exist. One must move through the conflictual, divided character of experience and not skip over it. A too-quick jump to unity is frequently achieved by asserting the experience of the dominant group in society as a universal.

This is particularly evident in the work of Schleiermacher himself. Schleiermacher's subordinationism leads him to distinguish between the work of God the "Father" in the world (creation) and the work of the "Son" in the church (redemption). The latter is purely spiritual. The church is "so spiritual a society." The spiritual God-consciousness of the church is effected through the work of the Holy Spirit "as something inward." The church gathered and sustained by this inward, spiritual bonding of the sanctifying Spirit is a place of peace and harmony.[21]

But this is exclusively the experience of a harmonious world view of German upper-middle-class males. The Holy Spirit operates to bond the church into a peaceful whole; this same spirit of bonding animates the civil order, "the common bent found in all who constitute together a moral personality, to seek the advancement of the whole."[22] Schleiermacher equated the "advanced" civilization of the Christian people with the blessing of God,[23] thereby labeling the third world as "uncivilized" and inharmonious.

This same equation is evident in modern liberals like Ferm, who are critical of liberation movements precisely because they disturb the smooth unity of the whole social enterprise. He speaks disapprovingly of black theologians who are "strident" and militant, such as James Cone and Joseph Washington, and favors those who are more "moderate." "Should black theology," asks Ferm, "be solely concerned with its own particular 'inner history,' or should it build bridges with the universal 'outer history' shared by all humankind?" Feminist theologians as well are chastised for "blatant reverse sexism."[24]

All these power struggles evaporate when the church is seen as a spiritual realm animated by a pacifying and harmonizing Spirit that has no independent identity apart from these relationships. This spiritual realm is divorced from the world and especially from conflicts in that world. Schleiermacher had a fine distaste for the "bodily side of the matter."[25] His liberal successors have adopted his distaste for messy, conflictual, and many-faceted historical reality.

The Spirit, subordinate to the "Father" and even to the "Son," confined to maintaining personal relationships with no independent identity of its own, sounds stereotypically feminine in the extreme when viewed in this light.

Jean Baker Miller quotes the following case of a woman who buys into this stereotypically feminine role in human affairs.

> Edith grew up the model of a "perfect female"; she was well instructed by her mother in how to win and please men. She did not know how to please herself, except by finding an attractive man with good prospects. Pretty and popular, she eventually married Bert, one of her most promising suitors. She became the super-wife and super-mother and came increasingly to rest her security on the belief that she could tie all of her family to her, not because they really loved and wanted her as herself, but because they surely needed her.

> She did so much for them and made life so good
> for them, how could they not? For a long time she
> prided herself on how indispensable she had be-
> come to everyone. This became almost the only
> source of her sense of identity.[26]

It bears repeating that a large part of the Miller thesis is that societies have "assigned" certain psychological responsibilities to women, such as the maintenance of relationships, and has continued to allow "mankind" to view itself as "self-seeking, competitive, aggressive and destructive,"[27] while support relationships were still maintained by women.

It is then not, perhaps, so curious that theologians have done the same to the Godhead. One aspect of God, an aspect deemed subordinate and peripheral, the Spirit, has been chosen to be responsible for self-giving and for sustaining relationships. But God the "Father" has remained the "Almighty": impassive, remote, and unknowable, dominating "his" creation.

In liberal theology, this relating quality of the Divine has often been stressed more, as in liberalism's emphasis on the divine immanence. But this has only resulted in a devaluation of God and especially God in Christ (note the liberal Jesus), for these same "feminized" qualities. They have been considered by the larger culture as confined to a private and interior realm, the spiritual, and are consequently divorced from the real business of history. Ann Douglas thus calls liberalism "the loss of Theology."

It is, therefore, necessary both to reclaim the co-equality and co-eternality of the Spirit with God the Creator and God the Redeemer in order to overcome the devaluation of these relational qualities of the

Spirit *and* to free the Spirit to act in history and not outside it.

The Relational Spirit

The foundation of a renewed doctrine of the Trinity and hence an appreciation of the role of the Holy Spirit as God is that God gives and receives, both as God relates with the Godhead (the immanent Trinity) and as God relates with the world (the economic Trinity). Dichotomizing these two has produced a theological deception where God's selfhood can be seen as somehow different and remote from God's action in the world. This is the result of a divisive, analytical approach in theology, which assumes that understanding comes from the reduction of ideas to their separate, component parts. On the contrary, insight often comes from the attempt to connect ideas creatively. Thus we must never fail to deal with the Trinity wholistically— God is and acts together.

In addition to a falsifying analytic, another theological problem that must be overcome in thinking about God as Trinity is the idea of the persons of the Trinity. In Karl Rahner's work, for example, the personhood of God is interpreted in "our secular use of the word person." But Rahner's interpretation of that use is a one-sided, narrow individualism that sees "person" as a completely distinguished center of activity, divorceable from other such centers of action. But there is another way of viewing person as represented in the work of such personalists as Buber, Rogers, Hölderlin, Feuerbach, Ebner, Rosenstock, and others, a way that denies there is any meaning to the concept of the isolated individual.

It is a puzzle that while study after study is compiled showing that personality does not develop in a societal vacuum, and that, in fact, a total lack of sociality from birth can even result in death from parental deprivation, humanity continues to operate from an abstractionist viewpoint that deems the independent, isolated individual a possibility. We operate this way in psychology, in sociology, in politics and theology, despite the complete absence of any empirical evidence that the wholly self-possessed, self-contained individual has ever existed.

It may be that we cling to the myth of the truly developed person as individual[28] because bonding between persons is seen culturally as a sign of dependence, as an admission of need, and hence as weak. Yet relatedness is not weakness, but a source of strength, as outgroups from the experience of the Israelities in Egypt, American revolutionaries (if we don't hang together, we all hang separately), to black Americans (black power), to the women's movement (sisterhood is powerful) have discovered. Frederick Herzog is particularly helpful here.

> Might it not be that only in a false arrangement of power we feel the need to "transcend" the self? It may well be that the self offers the appearance of separateness where human beings begin to lord it over one another, that is, where power is abused to divide humankind into persons and non-persons. In order to make a clear point here the Christian needs the Jewish understanding of Jesus' selfhood. This does not mean that this will immediately solve all problems. But there might just be a fighting chance that we finally will find a common ground of Scripture interpretation that

helps "the needed universalism" to emerge creatively. Christianity alone seems incapable of making the contribution humankind so sorely needs
today. Within our western tradition it will take a
concerted effort of seeking to recover our common
roots.[29]

Hence when human beings move from a paradigm of
exclusion and domination to one of inclusion and
equality, our notions of what it means to be a self can
change from isolated individualism to corporate selfhood.

This has profound implications for understanding
the corporate selfhood of God. The relatedness of the
Trinity does not remain a problem when the personhood of God is understood as fundamentally and in-
separably social. To be a person means *to be in relation.* Buber's dictum "in the beginning is the relation"
bears repeating here. The divine life is one of mutuality
and sharing precisely because person is a shared relation. This shared relatedness does not run the risk of
collapsing the Trinity into monotheism, since distinc-
tiveness and mutuality are not seen to threaten one
another. Tritheism is likewise ruled out, since it is non-
sense to talk about the personhood of deity as isolating
and isolatable.

But the consideration of the Trinity as person-in-
relation, fundamentally tied to the being of God in the
world, means that this relatedness is open to human
participation. God is a self-communicating God who
enters into a genuine relationship of reciprocity with
humanity. God gives and receives in interacting with
the human.

The combination of reciprocity in the divine life and

in the divine-human encounter needs to be explored as well. The presence of God in the world as Spirit is an interaction of God with social humanity. Paul Tillich notes, "The divine Spirit's invasion of the human spirit does not occur in isolated individuals but in social groups, since all the functions of the human spirit . . . are conditioned by the social content of the ego-thou encounter."[30] This social revelation is a serious challenge to charismatic spirituality and its isolating inwardness.

The sociology of divine revelation is central if we are going to deal at all effectively with the relation between God the Holy Spirit and Jesus whom we call the Christ. The Western Church has adopted a Christocentric bias that has resulted in a subordination of the Spirit and nearly everything else to this person Jesus. He is the Lord of history, the Messiah of Israel, the High Priest, and so forth. The Holy Spirit in traditional theology is the Spirit of Christ, determined by him.

The notion of corporate selfhood can help Christians begin to recognize the post-Pentecostal presence of the Holy Spirit in the people of God. This is to say that the Spirit is a genuine presence of God in human history that moves directly from the Jesus movement, never in contradiction to it, always in continuity from that moment to this, *but also beyond it.* Such an approach avoids notions of Christ as center, norm, and the like when these are understood as a once-for-all limitation on God. There is only one Christ, and there is only one Spirit. The Spirit does not displace Christ, but neither does "she" duplicate him. The Spirit is our understanding of the continued interaction of God with God and God with humanity.

This interaction is what Moltmann has called "an

eternal love affair between God and humanity."[31] The term Bridegroom both pointed to and obscured this interaction, as it expresses the divine/human relation in a heterosexist and patriarchal way. But the underlying mutuality that term fails sufficiently to illumine can be captured in a word such as lover; God and humanity are lovers.

The lover is constantly going out to the beloved to share his or her life. Pseudo-Dionysius wrote, "Love does not permit the lover to rest in himself [or herself]. It draws him [or her] out of himself [or herself] that he [or she] may be entirely in the beloved." When the beloved is suffering, the one who loves suffers too, because a lover cannot bear the suffering of the beloved. Hence, God—engaged in human struggles through loving humanity—suffers in this relationship.

In the history of the church, theologians have tried very hard to avoid patripassionism, the suffering of God. Compassion and sympathy in the deity was seen as a sign of weakness, unacceptable for the almighty Father. Women are seen as more appropriately compassionate (the Hebrew word for compassion is the same as that used for a mother's painful love for the child in her womb). But compassionate, suffering love is not weakness, in a stereotypically feminized view. On the contrary, it is a great strength. It is the ability to relate to another in love even to the point of personal sacrifice, the supreme quality we experience in our relationship with God whom we call the Christ.

It is precisely the concept of a crucified God that caused Moltmann to rethink the Trinitarian relationships.

That God suffered on the cross means that God is a self-giving God. The foundation of the Trinity is the idea that God gives and receives. This relational view is opposed to the monarchial view, which deems God self-sufficient and self-possessed.

The Spirit of Resistance

> If you love me, keep my commandments. I will ask the *Father* to give you another *resistance counselor* to be with you forever—the Spirit of truth. The world cannot share in *him* because it neither sees nor knows *him*. But you know *him* because *he* remains with you and is in you. I will not leave you orphaned.
>
> —John 14:15-18, HERZOG[32]

Frederick Herzog has translated *Paraklētos* as resistance counselor. Counselor, comforter, or sanctifier, other translations found of *Paraklētos*, demonstrate the difference in his interpretative perspective.

Counselor, comforter, or sanctifier as translations for *Paraklētos* demonstrate a view of history as harmonious and unitary. The coming of the Spirit and his or her action are not seen to disturb things as they are, but rather to complement them. Or, in times of trouble, the action of the Spirit enables humans to adjust to their problems.

Herzog's translation reflects a view of history as an arena of conflict in which to be a Christian means having to resist things as they are and struggle for change. The Spirit, comments Herzog, "is the resistance counselor who helps the disciple resist the claims of secularity." The coming of the Spirit is seen by him as the infusion "of a power that principally wants man [the disciple] to resist."[33]

As one contemporary social critic has observed, resistance can thus be seen as the presence of the Spirit:

"To resist is to become fully alive, truly alive for the first time. It is to say not only will I not accept what you are doing, I will stop you from doing it."[34]

Jesus' life is frequently painted as a pacific pastoral of a simple carpenter who turned the other cheek. While Jesus may have turned the other cheek when struck, he kept right on going and doing what he thought God wanted him to do. This conviction even led him actively to resist buying and selling in the house of God.

For the sake of liberation
Jesus showed himself to be free
vis-à-vis religious traditions
that were oppressing people,
contrary to God's will.
He confronted the pious people
who were using God as an alibi
for not seeing human beings and their needs
and for not heeding the demands of justice.
Jesus' God is the Father of infinite goodness
who treasures the poor,
the lost drachma,
the stray sheep
and the prodigal son.
The worship that pleases God most
is service rendered to others,
and particularly to the lowliest ones
in whom God has hidden himself.
Jesus' prophetic criticism also attacks the powerful,
those who enjoy a monopoly
over possessions, knowledge and power.
Jesus does not speak in terms of their interests,
but rather in terms of the interests and
yearnings of the poor.
All this scandalized many,
and they got together to get rid of Jesus.[35]

It surprises so many to discover that Jesus was in fact born of the poor in Israel, was an illiterate outsider to the religious establishment, and was finally executed as a political subversive, that one must ask whether some filtering process causes these essentials of his life and ministry as one of resistance to the powers that be to be read out. A closer examination of such interpretation reveals that often a framework of meaning is operative which deems that all "religious" or "spiritual" things are out of this world. The poor become the poor in spirit, not the poor in fact. The author of the Moffatt Bible Commentary writes:

> On Jesus' lips the "good news" has a purely religious import. . . . The term *the poor* is to be taken in its inward, *spiritual* sense . . . and similarly the expressions *captive, blind, oppressed* indicate not primarily the down-trodden victims of material force, such as Rome's, but the victims of inward repressions, neuroses, and other spiritual ills due to misdirection and failure of life's energy and purpose.[36]

Presumably a Jesus engaged merely in helping the Israelites be better adjusted and less neurotic would not have disturbed the Roman authorities. On the contrary, better-adjusted populations are easier to rule. Jesus was clearly not a pastoral counselor, but one in the prophetic line who denounced injustice and oppression on behalf of the poor *in fact*, not *in spirit*.

This contrast between "in fact" and "in spirit" raises the point at issue. Is salvation something that happens in history, *in fact*, or something that happens outside history, in a numinous and undefined place generally labeled the spiritual realm?

Salvation must begin in intrahistorical reality to have any connection with God's acts in history from creation through the exodus to the incarnation and beyond. Hence the Spirit is not outside history any more than Jesus was outside history. The Spirit is related to Jesus of Nazareth, the one who resisted even to the point of death, in an intrahistorical sense. As Jesus was one resistance counselor, so the Spirit is another (John 14:16).

The action of the Spirit in traditional Trinitarian terms is changed as it confronts the view that history is active and conflictual and not static and harmonious. The Spirit as sanctifier or comforter as it comes to the poor today helps them to perceive their situation of oppression and injustice as wrong.

The idea that history is changing and conflictual leads to the conclusion that it is *changeable* by human action. Sanctification happens within history, within the political realm. To "comfort" the poor thus means changing their situation and working to eliminate the conditions that keep them poor. It is a recognition that the economic reality is that some people are poor *in order that* some other people can remain rich and get richer. It is the realization that in the text "The poor you always have with you [John 12:8]," the emphasis should fall on the word "with," as in "solidarity with." In a harmonious view of history, that text has been read as a passive acceptance of certain givens, i.e., that some will always be poor. Or, worse, the text is misread, "Be sure you keep some people poor."

But it is also the case that "comforting the poor" is patronizing and paternalistic. The poor determine their own resistance and accept responsibility for it. Paulo Freire has written:

The oppressed, who have been shaped by the death-affirming climate of oppression, must find through their struggle the way to life-affirming humanization, which does not lie *simply* in having more to eat (although it does involve having more to eat and cannot fail to include this aspect). The oppressed have been destroyed precisely because their situation has reduced them to things. In order to regain their humanity they must cease to be things and fight as men [and women].[37]

The spirit of resistance is present where life is overcoming death, where human struggle is going on.

Dorothee Soelle has written powerfully and effectively of the problems of the first world in responding to liberation themes.[38] She looks at resistance as a category for those in the first world who "are caught by the basic capitalistic experiences of powerlessness, determination from the outside, uncontrollability of life. We do need resistance over against the prevailing experience and ideology mutually enforced."[39]

Yet Soelle is also critical of the adequacy of the term for the first world, since a theology of resistance participates in Protestant pessimism and its mistrust of human nature and of the eschatological meaning of history. There is a certain opposition to the theology of liberation and its Catholic tradition of cooperation. She gives several examples: Gustav Heinemann, an active member of the German Confessing Church in its resistance to Hitler, in his last conversation before his death reported that the only real hope remaining, as he saw it, was the return of Christ and the end of history and human efforts; Daniel Berrigan is cited for his insistence on resistance. In a lecture, Berrigan "didn't let himself be touched by our questions about success, about allies, about strategies."[40]

The Sojourners Community and the Center for Creative Non-Violence are noted for their "lack of hope in any mass movement."[41] Resistance, therefore, may not adequately describe the vision necessary for those in the first world to overcome Protestant pessimism and find a sustaining hope that demands change.

The Spirit of Justice

Justice may be a theological description more appropriate to the action of the Spirit in the first world, in which the church is not, by and large, the poor themselves, but those who are enmeshed in structures that keep others poor. The Spirit of Justice makes possible the shock of recognition of the pain of the other. But, as Paulo Freire has pointed out, it does not stop there: "Discovering oneself to be an oppressor may cause considerable anguish, but it does not necessarily lead to solidarity with the oppressed."[42] Solidarity means entering into the situation of the oppressed and acknowledging the injustice of that situation. It is a conversion to the other.

It is necessary to discover what kind of justice the Spirit of God embodies. Justice, in the biblical materials, is not the Enlightenment model of a reasonable ethic based on an equal distribution of rights. In North America the Protestant Church's understanding of social justice has been shaped partially, if not wholly, by a cultural understanding of what justice means. Justice is fair play, it is equal access to inalienable rights: life, liberty, and the pursuit of happiness.

John Rawls, in his recent work *A Theory of Justice*, proposes that a modern theory of social justice would emerge as an answer to the question, "What principles of social justice would free and rational persons accept if they chose principles in a situation of genuine equality?" His answer is that social justice is to be conceived as "fairness."[43]

By contrast, the image of justice presented in the biblical narratives is mostly unfair and remarkably biased. The ordering of God's relationship to Israel begins with Exodus and God's faithfulness to Israel in that experience. By designating that rag-tag band of slaves as the chosen of God, God is revealed as one who sides with those who are out of power. Egypt was an imperial community; by contrast, Israel is called to develop a different kind of community with a different or alternative consciousness of human values. The economic order is to be ordered by the Jubilee, a fifty-year period after which all accumulated property reverts to its original owners, in which slaves are freed and indentured servants relieved of their debts. The "year of the Sovereign" is a reminder that possession is a temporary matter; that all belongs to Yahweh requires that possessions be distributed approximately equally among the people of the community.

The purpose of Jubilee is to redress the imbalance that inevitably results in community (see Leviticus 25:8-55). While it is doubtful that the Jubilee year ever took place in actual fact, and one can readily see why no community leaders would initiate it, its existence in scripture is an important image of the divine view of social and economic justice. Biblical justice is a decidedly unfair bias in favor of the poor.

The Spirit brings God's justice, not clever courtroom legalisms. This is the justice of the one who cares deeply about the poor and oppressed and is on their side. This Spirit Justice means that the white, middle-class church is confronted in its affluence, its racism, its sexism.

For this white, middle-class, North American Protestant Church to take on the metaphor of the Poor means conversion to the poor, a letting go of status and privilege in order to be in solidarity with the powerless. The poor are those who are out of power, and the church is converted to the poor when it takes on this self-definition, when it is converted by the Spirit of Justice to the God who is out of power. The suffering God is present in the suffering of the poor and only present in a church that is with the poor.

The North American white Protestant Church needs to hear a pneumatology of Justice in order to take on an identity, not as the poor but with the poor. "The poor you will have with you always." This identity must overcome denominational insularity as private associations in order to enter into the realm of history, the political realm. It is always within history that we find the Spirit of Justice working out the task of salvation, and it is always within history that we take on the task of the church to do justice.

The metaphors of the Body of Christ and the Poor challenge the North American Protestant Church to be an interdenominational, public, political church. This church already exists in fragmentary ways within the women's movement in the churches and the nuclear freeze movement, and it is to these concrete situations that we turn to find connections with these metaphors.

Chapter 5 LOCATIONS

The Women's Movement

ONE of the most crucial ecclesiological questions we face as Protestants is our divisions into denominations and from one another as Protestant and Catholic Christians. One experience of unity that goes against this divisiveness is that of the women's movement. The real location of the ecumenical movement, in contrast to ecumenism's currently sputtering academic efforts, may be that of the women's movement in the churches.

The Association of Theological Schools' *Fact Book on Theological Education* shows 8,972 women enrolled in 193 schools in the United States and Canada, making up 20 percent of the total number of students in this type of institution. The greatest increases in numbers of women were in programs leading to ordination.

Between 1972 and 1978, there was an increase of 269.6 percent.

Between 1977, when women were first admitted to the Episcopal priesthood, and 1981, 438 women have been ordained in that denomination. Mainline Protestant denominations have a total of 3,200 women clergy. While this represents only 3 percent of the total clergy in the United States, it is an increase (over the same period of time) of more than 300 percent![1]

Roman Catholic women have greatly expanded their ministries in recent years. A decline in the number of male priests has created a shortage. Women, both lay and "religious," have developed numerous styles of ministry in order to fill these gaps.

Yet this dramatic increase in total numbers masks the problem that all these women are still marginal in terms of power.

For Protestant women, placement is a crucial issue. The following is a summary of a study completed in 1979 of women's placement in American Baptist churches.

> The survey of ministerial candidates indicated that most women who sought placement in ministry were successful. However, each segment of the placement/recruitment system clearly appears to have been more responsive to men candidates than to women. There is evidence of discrimination in seminaries, among executive and area ministers, among pulpit committee representatives, and among the laity in general. The women candidates perceive themselves as being less accepted as ministers than men. Furthermore, the number of contacts they have, the salary and allowances they enjoy, and the amount of time it takes for them to be placed indicates that the problem is not just with the women's perceptions but

indeed does reside in virtually all segments of the recruitment/placement system itself.[2]

It takes twice as long for a woman to find a job as for a man. She can expect an average of $3,000 less in annual salary than her male colleagues, and her total travel and study allowance averages half that of a comparable male minister.

Women faculty in seminaries have begun to appear, but they are also at the periphery of power. There are forty-seven women faculty at mainline Protestant and Catholic seminaries in the United States, out of a total of 827. Most of these women faculty are untenured and of junior rank. In fact, there are only twelve women who are full professors at any seminary. Many women work part time, or in combined administrative and teaching posts. While 15.9 percent of seminary administrators are women, sixty-three women, or nearly 58 percent, are registrars. Only two women are deans of seminaries.

No woman heads a major denomination. Very few denominations have any senior administrators who are women. Women in parish settings are usually scattered and without effective collegial support.

This situation of shared powerlessness unites women. The women's movement in the churches exists where, as the Catholic feminist theologian of liberation Mary Elizabeth Hunt has observed, one never thinks to ask another woman whether she is Protestant or Catholic, Lutheran, or Episcopalian. That is the least of the problems.

In an article titled "Women Ministering in Mutuality: The Real Connections," one real connection for Hunt is women—expressed for her, and perhaps for all of us, in women's music. Hunt quotes Carole Etzler, whose song "Sometimes I Wish" expresses women's torment as they see "all of the pain and the hurt and the longing of my sisters and me as we try to be free."[3]

Hunt makes a real connection as she finds "support among many Protestant women in ministry, whose lives answer some of the questions we have about combining commitment to ministry with family and relational life."[4] These connections include "the bond between so-called lay women and religious women." The women are drawn together because in a church structured by patriarchy "all women are lay women"; but, she affirms, "all women are religious women."[5] That is to say, lay and "religious" women in the Roman Catholic Church are both alienated from the clerical establishment. Part of their identity as Roman Catholic women stems from that exclusion, as does part of their sense of mutuality.

Two points need to be made in connection with the "real connection." The women's movement in the churches is not without its share of problems and genuine conflicts. The movement includes many different kinds of women, who approach their situations in many different ways. This issue is discussed frankly and openly by Letitia Brennan in her article "Conflict and Cooperation Among Women in the Roman Catholic Church." Brennan quotes Sister Teresa Kane, who received many hostile responses, particularly from women, to her challenge to John Paul II during his American tour "to be open to and respond to the voices coming from the women of this country who are desirous of serving in and through the Church as fully participating members."[6]

Sister Teresa subsequently wrote to her colleagues, the members of the Executive Board of the Leadership Conference of Religious Women, that the hostile, unchristian and uncharitable expressions which have come forth from so many of the faithful—clergy, religious, laity—are a deep source of concern to me and have caused me to reflect upon the violence which is so present in the human spirit.[7]

Women do not cease being human in the movement. The structures of patriarchy are designed to keep women apart and to ensure that women who attain positions of leadership and power do so at the price of solidarity with other women. As Mary Elizabeth Hunt has remarked, "On the social scene—moves up the social ladder are always accomplished by stepping on human rungs."[8]

Protestant women are divided among themselves as well. When women clergy of the United Church of Christ met in 1979 and voted to support the ordination of gay and lesbian individuals to the ministry, several women vigorously dissented, claiming concern over the effect such actions would have "with regard to the calling of women pastors." Actions such as these and their coverage in the national press were believed to "add to unwarranted concern about women serving as pastors."[9] Here solidarity with another oppressed group, some of whom are women, is believed to imperil the precarious status that the few women who have managed to be ordained appear to have achieved. It is the type of divide-and-conquer motif that keeps women apart and unfocused about the real problems they face. But the real connections persist. In Detroit in 1975, and in Baltimore in 1978, a total of nearly 3,500 women addressed the issues surrounding the ordination of women in the Roman Catholic Church. Washington, DC, was the scene in 1981 of "Women Moving Church," a conference designed to identify and create resources for empowerment for all women in the church.

As a Protestant participant in these conferences, I became aware that what is being sought through this movement is not primarily the ordination of Roman Catholic women to the priesthood. Protestant women clergy know full well that ordination is the beginning of sexism in the church, so to speak, and not its end. What is sought by Roman Catholic laywomen and "religious," and Protestant women, both clergy and lay, is fundamentally a new church. Mary Elizabeth Hunt said in Baltimore that this change in the church

> will result not simply in equality, but in new forms of mutuality. We are seeking, not some form of ecclesiastical ERA, but a complete structural change which turns the power model upside down by giving those who have been excluded, women, Blacks, gay people, the poor, equal voice in the Church.[10]

Thus the situation of women in the church must be seen to transcend their differences in particular traditions. This unity does exist, not only despite their diversity, but by necessity including their diversity.

It is, therefore, totally false to the nature of the problem of disunity among the churches to make the ordination of women appear to be a stumbling block to the union of churches. That women are ordained by some communions and not by others has been noted time and again in the World Council of Churches as an impediment to unity. It was not, in fact, until 1979 at the Consultation on Ordination of Women in Ecumenical Perspective at Chateau Klingen near Strasbourg that the "problem of women and unity was posed as a 'possibility.' "[11]

Letty Russell, in her report on this consultation, refers to what she calls the "Strasbourg shift." At the Strasbourg meeting, there was a shift from a "paradigm of domination" to a "paradigm of cooperation." In the latter view, women become partners in the journey for unity, and not objectified obstacles on the path toward unity.

A paradigm of domination is one in which the unification of communions is regarded "as a process of *ordering faith* so that we can all fit together." Nontheological issues such as "culture, nationality, economic status, race, and (a late-comer to the list) sex" must be excluded or the order in process would become completely unmanageable.[12]

One thinks here of 2 Peter and the domestic codes. Unity becomes a matter of discipline and compromise, and those compromised and kept in line are those already marginal to the dominant consensus.

But a paradigm of cooperation allows us to rethink the ecumenical task as a journey that is "a process of *discovering faith* on the way to . . . 'the end of the earth' (Acts 1:8)."[13] Marginalized persons, like women, may then be able to contribute to theological discussions insights into new dimensions of unity. What happens when the membership opens up is not theological chaos. "All of a sudden the unity of humankind is not a theological topic," observes Russell, "but rather an existential reality as the 'outsiders' share in the journey."[14]

In this view of reality, women's lived experience of the possibility of bonding across denominational, class, and racial lines shows the possibility of new human bonding of which all are potentially capable.

Thus, women are not a problem for ecumenical discussion. They are one of the few real possibilities remaining in ecumenism.

Another study of structure in the church is the working paper of the Commission on Faith and Order of the National Council of the Churches of Christ, "Authority-in-Community."[15] It is an attempt to address the tensions arising from the drive for equality in leadership in the church and in the family and to reflect theologically on this question of authority from the perspective of God's preference for the dominated. The process by which the paper itself was produced is very similar to that of *Your Daughters Shall Prophesy: Feminist Alternatives in Theological Education,* by The Cornwall Collective[16]; though it was actually written by one person, Madeline Boucher, it expresses the ideas of the two full days of discussion by the participants at the NCCC meeting.

In the paper, authority and power are described in their relationship to community: "*Power* is the ability to implement action, to bring about an effect, sometimes a change. *Authority* is the right to claim or exercise power."[17] Many people have viewed power and authority as primarily masculine traits, understood in a paradigm of male = authority/domination, versus female = powerlessness/submissiveness. But in many forms and images, the biblical witness, "far from establishing an order of domination-subordination," points out that "the reign of God overthrows such a system and establishes a new social order."[18]

This new order is not one that simply reverses the groups on the top and bottom, but one in which power and authority are exercised as leaven, and as servanthood. This is empowerment and accountability in community. The church's vocation, according to this working paper, is "nothing less than to be a sign and instrument of such a new order—an order which may be described as authority *in*, not *over*, community."[19]

Women and Racism

It is nevertheless true that in the realm of the actual, the women's movement in the churches is very largely a white women's movement. In the last few pages of this book nearly every mention of women's unity or women's potential or even women's conflict should be modified by the adjective white. Racism, as a white problem in white-dominated Western culture, is imported into the women's movement.

This has been the source of more than one confrontation between women, and is never less painful the more frequently it is replayed. But here again the issue must become the total perspective—in fact, a paradigm shift. A world view that sees whiteness as a definition of Western culture and assumes the superiority of that culture fundamentally undermines feminism and the possibilities the women's movement can open up.

White women are frequently involved in being "sure to include some black women" on their conference programs, ignoring the fact that an agenda set by whites may not include all the issues black women need to address. This becomes especially insidious when it is racism that is to be examined, and white women import black women to talk about the "problem," as though racism were a black problem.[20]

Here, in raw detail, the racial divisions among us in North America are exposed, revealing a distorted sense of ourselves as North Americans and a distorted sense of history. But this same exposure can reveal to us how essential racial inclusivity is to the existence of the church for women as well as for men.

The racially exclusive character of the women's movement in the churches and the ways in which white women are currently struggling to deal with this problem again points to possibility. The Women's Theological Coalition of Boston-area seminaries has self-consciously been in the process of attempting to deal with its racism and the institutional racism of its member schools. As part of this, the Anna Howard Shaw Center, a women's research and resources center at the Boston University School of Theology, has searched for years for a minority director.

The Women's Theological Center, currently located in the Boston area, is an experiment in feminist theological education. The design of the center is to provide for a "community of racial, ethnic, economic, national, and ecumenical diversity, in which women can build on and develop the skills, experience, and theological and analytical perspective which will enable them to be more effective ministers and agents of social and ecclesial change."[21] From its earliest stages and planning, minority women have been involved in this program of theological education, and their needs and concerns are at its center.

This model for unity is one of self-examination and institutional examination. But owning one's private and institutional racism has been decried as a barrier to unity. The attempt to form interethnic coalitions, however, has been criticized as an attempt to homogenize the identity of ethnic groups in order to co-opt them.

In a vivid discussion at the American Academy of Religion annual meeting in 1981, Thomas Hoyt, a black biblical theologian at Hartford Seminary, made this perceptive observation.

We need to be attuned to the implications for a shared cultural outlook. In the affirmations of T.S. Eliot, the only educated person is one who has mastered a second language. This means that one's indigenous culture with its symbols needs to be exposed to another's and the other's fully appreciated. That is why without heterogeneous dialogue we see through a homogenous prism which does not encompass the world view or perspective of others.[22]

Without interethnic coalition, individuals from the same culture effectively end up talking only to themselves. But participants are not asked to submerge their identity in the whole. Instead, in Hoyt's terms, they are asked to learn a *second* language. One does not colonize one's first language as the price of unity.

The women's movement in the churches dares not be a white women's movement; the churches dare not be white churches. But neither can they be allowed to become racially mixed, but white-defined. They must hold, as does the women's movement, to the metaphors of Body, but must also take on the metaphor of the Poor by identifying with those out of power in terms of race and class, as well as of sex.

THE PEACE MOVEMENT

THE peace movement in the churches exhibits some of the same possibilities as well as some of the same problems as the women's movement. The existence of the peace movement in the churches demonstrates the potential for bonding, but racial, sexual, and class barriers still remain.

The Freeze Movement in the Churches

The nuclear freeze movement in its most basic form calls for a halt to the testing, development, and production of nuclear weapons by the United States and the Soviet Union, followed by negotiations to reduce the nuclear arsenals of both countries. This form of the freeze was initiated by Randall Forsberg, director of the Brookline, Massachusetts-based Institute for Defense and Disarmament Studies. Since the spring of 1981, when a scattering of New England town meetings voted to endorse a resolution drawn up by military analyst and peace activist Forsberg, the freeze movement has been endorsed by (post-November 1982 general elections) 307 city councils; 446 New England town meetings; 61 county councils; the state legislatures of Massachusetts, Oregon, Connecticut, Vermont, Maine, Minnesota, Wisconsin, Hawaii, Delaware, Iowa, and New York; the Kansas and Pennsylvania houses of representatives; the California State Assembly; and the Alaska, Maryland, and Illinois senates. According to a May 1982 poll taken by *The New York Times*, 87 percent of the population favors a nuclear freeze that would give neither the United States nor the Soviet Union a military advantage. In June 1982 nearly one million Americans demonstrated for peace at the Second Special Session on Disarmament of the United Nations in New York. There is good reason to assume that the nuclear freeze movement represents a populist movement without precedent in American history.

American Protestant denominations that are predominantly white have responded to and participated in this movement to an astonishingly great degree. In the Episcopal Church, the House of Bishops issued its first unanimous pastoral letter on a controversial social issue in 1981, pledging to fast one day a week, engage in prayer, and raise the issue of the arms race and arms reduction in their pastoral work. Peace commissions, some of which have paid directors, have been established in the majority of dioceses. In September of 1982 at the General Convention in New Orleans, a stronger statement was made by the bishops. It condemned the spiraling buildup in arms, it called for a freeze on development, testing, and deployment of nuclear weapons and for a mutually assured reduction of arms, and it urged the Episcopal Church to place this issue at the center of its attention. This issue was made a focus of programming for the next three years, with $125,000 allotted per year for staff. In addition, a series of resolutions supported by a minority of bishops questioned the concept of deterrence and any use of nuclear weapons.

Both Presbyterian denominations have moved toward peace programming, with an intention to combine peace programs in their unification efforts (as other social programs are being combined). The United Presbyterian Church, in addition to supporting the freeze and educational programs for peace, has made understanding the Soviet Union a focus. It is leading a trip in 1983 to the Soviet Union for synod leaders of peace groups and other national church leaders for the purpose of meeting with Soviet church and governmental leaders.

The Presbyterian Church in the United States pledged at its annual meeting to work for peace. In addition to a $75,000 per year inheritance the church has received for peace work, the Presbyterian Church U.S. has pledged an annual gift of $1 million to be used for education at the synod, and on national and local levels.

The United Church of Christ at its 1981 General Synod adopted a resolution calling on the United Church of Christ to become a peace church. The nature of the church is Christ, the resolution argued, and Christ's church in the world should be a church of peacemaking. Its right to be the church is based on its commitment to peace. The General Synod established a Peace Theology Development Team, which has as its job to define "the theological base for considering the UCC to be a Peace Church at this point in history," to elaborate public policy consistent with this theological base, and to propose new structure and program capability needs to give expression to these theological commitments. This task was reaffirmed at General Synod XIV.

The United Methodists voted at their quadrennial General Conference to take an annual peace offering to make peace a focus of that denomination. This focus had been around hunger and development, and peace was added to that concern.

The Southern Baptists have taken a slightly different approach. They have started peace fellowship groups in local parishes, using the Church of the Savior (Washington, DC) World Peace-Makers fellowship as their model. These groups will combine prayer, study, and action.

The American Baptists at their National Conference in 1982 made peace an issue of top priority and focus.

Three Lutheran denominations, the Lutheran Church in America, the American Lutheran Church, and the American Evangelical Lutheran Church, all voted at their annual meetings in 1982 to support a verifiable nuclear freeze. These denominations are currently moving toward union, and the peace issue has been made a prime focus in the planning for union, as have several other social issues.

The traditional black denominations, such as the African Methodist Episcopal Zion Church, the African Methodist Episcopal Church, and the National Baptist Convention, have not been as active on the peace issue. This reluctance to work on a national, public level (efforts on local levels notwithstanding) may come from several places. The black movement in America has a recollection of the negative reception to Martin Luther King and his move to peace issues in the last years of his life. In his last-published book, *Where Do We Go from Here: Chaos or Community?* King focused on the disproportionately high number of black men dying in Vietnam and made the economic connection that the cost of the war was retarding black liberation at home: "The security we profess to seek in foreign adventures we will lose in our decaying cities. The bombs in Vietnam explode at home; they destroy the hopes and possibilities for a decent America."[23]

Opposition to the war was unpopular not only in the white community, but also in segments of the black community, and co-workers such as Andrew Young were convinced that King had taken a wrong turn in making the war a focus.

In addition, there are survival issues at stake in the black community in the current economic climate—employment, education, health care—that take tremendous time and energy. The lack of focus on the peace issue may also come from attention to pressing problems elsewhere. The systemic violence of racism is a day-to-day concern.

But there is still the issue of the extent to which the peace movement is a white-defined movement and is avoided by the black denominations for that reason. The question remains whether the white church has failed to make explicit the issue that King raised in 1967: military buildups threaten the economic survival of the black community to a greater degree than the white community. Racial justice should be at the heart of peace concerns.

PRIVATE AND PUBLIC CHURCH

THE Protestant denominational pattern of response and participation in the nuclear weapons freeze movement demonstrates the privatized, associational model, which, as has been noted, is typical of North American mainline Protestantism. Each denomination is hermetically sealed from the others to a large degree; all have some degree of involvement, but this is primarily directed at each denomination's own members. The churches are divided and prevented from making a concerted, direct political statement that would challenge the arms buildup on a public, political level.

Precisely because the Roman Catholic Church sees itself as a public institution (see the Christendom mentality discussion on pages 47-56), it is the Christian body within North America that has taken such a public, political stand. "The Challenge of Peace: God's Promise and Our Response" is a pastoral letter to the nation's 51 million Roman Catholic bishops. While pastoral letters are intended to advise Roman Catholics on moral courses of action and are not binding rules of the Catholic Church, a draft of the letter was made public several days prior to the November 1982 elections, in which nuclear freeze resolutions were on the ballot in nine states.

The first draft of the letter was circulated to the 285

American bishops in June 1982. Defense Secretary Caspar Weinberger and National Security Adviser William Clark both wrote detailed objections in response to the letter. Both were particularly critical of the no-first-use arguments contained in that draft. Weinberger wrote, "Were NATO to forego the possibility of a nuclear response to armed aggression, the Warsaw Pact might conclude that the risks of conventional attack against Western Europe were acceptable." Clark objected, "To deter effectively, we must make it clear to the Soviet leadership that we have the capability to, and will, respond to aggression."[24] The Administration clearly perceives that the bishops' letter is a political act and have responded in kind.

The third and final draft of the letter was approved overwhelmingly (238-9) by the American Catholic bishops at their May 1983 meeting in Chicago. Revisions of the second draft, notably a change from "halt" to "curb" in the call for "support for immediate, bilateral, verifiable, agreements to halt the testing, production and deployment of new weapon systems,"[25] had led former critics such as Weinberger to declare the revised version of the third draft "consistent with government policy." The bishops, in their overwhelmingly approved final version, returned to the stronger language and called for a halt.[26]

The final draft declares "we must continually say 'no' to nuclear war." Deterrence strategy must be reevaluated in light of this "no." Deterrence therefore is seen only as "a step on the way toward progressive disarmament." Each addition to a strategic posture must be "assessed in light of whether it will render steps toward 'progressive disarmament' more or less likely."

The limitation on the application of deterrence calls into question the threat to civilian populations, which effectively rules out the use of large-scale weapons because their enormous lethal capacity cannot be limited to military targets. This counters the American strategic option known as "counter-value," a code-phrase for the acceptability of targeting political, economic, and military institutions in or near urban areas. The bishops categorically state, "Under no circumstances may nuclear weapons or other instruments of mass slaughter be used for the purpose of destroying population centers or other predominantly civilian targets." The letter further assails U.S. governmental ability to compel obedience of Roman Catholic soldiers: "No Christian can rightfully carry out orders or policies deliberately aimed at killing noncombatants."

The letter takes specific stands on many other areas of U.S. policy. The bishops assail tactical nuclear weapons based in Europe because they present "an unacceptable moral risk" of escalating a conventional confrontation into a nuclear war that could not be contained. The MX missile is similarly a point of objection, since its very existence is destabilizing and might provoke a preemptive attack. Thus the bishops forthrightly declare "our support of a 'No First Use' Policy."

The letter, while specific, is a theological presentation of a "Gospel vision of peace." Nuclear weapons "threaten the very creative work of God among us."[27] The biblical vision of peace, the bishops' letter says, demands that "we must continually say no to the idea of nuclear war."

There remain many problems with the bishops' position.[28] The contents of the letter may represent only a minority of Catholics' views on nuclear war—the hierarchicalism of the Roman Catholic Church, while having the advantage of concerted action, has the disadvantage of appearing unilateral. Yet what is significant is the perception of this action by the Roman Catholic bishops on the part of the Republican administration as a political challenge with broadbased consequences, which must be met at the political level.

This is not to say that Protestants have never combined to issue a concerted statement on anything. Through their national body, the National Council of the Churches of Christ, the Protestant churches have acted in concert. An example is the Dun Commission Report, issued by the then-named Federal Council of Churches from a group that included Angus Dun, Reinhold Niebuhr, Paul Tillich, John C. Bennett, Walter Horton, Albert T. Mollegen, James Nichols, George F. Thomas, Georgia Harkness, and Robert L. Calhoun. The report supported nuclear buildup in the face of the cold war, calling on Christians "to support the policies of armament and preparedness and of taxation and consumption restraints required for the maintenance of adequate strength in the free world." The Dun Commission explicitly did not distinguish conventional weapons from nuclear weaponry, supported deterrence in an ideology of the "free world," and justified the use of nuclear weapons in furthering the cause of freedom. Georgia Harkness refused to sign the report because it caricatured pacifism; Robert Calhoun also refused to sign because the report exhibited confusion between Christian conscience and military necessity.[29]

While intended as a public statement, the Dun Commission Report reflects the cultural captivity of Protestantism at the time it was issued. The commission supported the buildup of nuclear arms and the prevailing ideology of deterrence. The overarching significance of the bishops' letter, by contrast, is its *dissent*. Thomas Fox, the editor of the *National Catholic Reporter*, believes that "The Challenge of Peace" will place U.S. Catholics in a confrontation with American policies, thereby forcing Catholics to make a choice between abiding by the moral teachings of the Catholic Church or supporting their government as defined by the Reagan administration. There is the potential for the greatest religious-political clash in U.S. history.[30]

The point is not that dissent per se is right, but that a distinctive stand was taken on the part of a church that understands itself as church and not as a private association. How can Protestants achieve a public, political consciousness of themselves as *church* while retaining the more horizontal, inclusive character their various polities do represent, in theory if not always in practice?

Here the lesson of the women's movement, that the personal is the political, is central. Women both within and without the church have attained an awareness that there is no exclusively private sphere, but that there are inextricable and reciprocal ties between one's private relationships and the larger social and political spheres. Hence they have given the metaphor of the Body of Christ concrete social and political reality. The relational Christ whose Body we form exists when we come together, informed by a paradigm of cooperation. We Christians can thus claim our corporate selfhood, meaning that we understand ourselves as taking on the historical task—becoming agents in history. In so doing, we attest that there can be no real separation between the individual and the social self. The self is formed only in community. Likewise, the church comes to an awareness of itself as a social entity—as part of culture. And, likewise, the social selfhood of the church is achieved when the church as a Body recognizes and takes responsibility for history, ceasing to scapegoat women, black people, Jews, or the so-called Third World. This corporate self means that ecumenism is a most radical political act—when the church not only claims to be but acts as the Body of Christ in solidarity with the poor.

RACISM IN THE PEACE MOVEMENT

THIS corporate self does not have as its model the bourgeois self, preoccupied with its own existence. The Body of Christ can never be separated in a culture of affluence from the metaphor of the Poor or it will be co-opted into supporting the status quo. This is the lesson of white domination of the nuclear freeze movement in the United States. The connections are not being made to the black church and black Americans that the nuclear buildup has profoundly racist consequences—the cutting of social welfare expenditures, which disproportionately affects the black community and which retards even the minor economic gains black Americans have made.

It may be an accurate perception on the part of black Americans that the energy devoted to the freeze movement is motivated by a desire primarily to save white skins. The nuclear freeze movement is nevertheless energized by the perception that the arms race may end the human race, irrespective of color or social class.

Can the churches, perhaps, make the connection that what they are about is not only peace—which translates for blacks into keeping things the way they are (minus the threat of war)—but peace*making*?

Peacemaking as a theological first step would involve a recognition of Dom Helder Camara's well-known spiral of violence. The oppression by economic and social institutions of those at the bottom of the power structures of this society is itself violence. Establishing justice in these violently repressive situations means, perhaps, precipitating conflict with the forces that are constantly operating to keep poverty in its place. In a harmonious view of history, challenges to systemic violence may appear to be in themselves violent and hence are not consistent with the demand for peace. But when it is recognized that, on the contrary, history is a scene of conflict and disharmony between social classes, then a theology of peacemaking can expand to entail that establishing peace means struggling for justice.

At the heart of the women's movement has been a claiming of conflict and a desire to move suppressed and hidden conflicts in human interaction into the open. Forced into restrictive and humanly stifling roles, women have labored for a long time under religious, social, and psychological pressures that a calm and serene acceptance of women's subservient role was their destiny; hence a refusal to submit was variously labeled sinful or neurotic, depending on the cultural ethos.

In breaking through these myths, women have been perceived as very angry. When women have come to a place where they can claim this anger as a true and correct response to oppression, they have been able to work through these myths to new self-definitions. This has resulted in a new appreciation of the necessity of dealing straightforwardly and honestly with conflict and claiming one's anger. Jean Baker Miller has contributed to the astonishingly important insight that war is an attempt to suppress conflict, to suppress dissent, and to force one group's views on another.[31] A recognition of the conflictual nature of reality and a forging of structures that will tolerate dissent without violence is a crucial lesson here.

Black churches are not involved in the peace movement because the connection between establishing peace and establishing justice has not been made forcefully enough. Yet the statistics are there. The world is spending $1 million a *minute* on military personnel and hardware. In thirty-two countries, governments spend more for the military than for education and health combined. In the United States, the richest superpower, one person in seven lives below the poverty level. The richest fifth of the world's population has 71 percent of the world's product; the poorest fifth has 2 percent.[32]

A public, political church may challenge the arms race, but without a sense of itself as with the poor, with those who are left with 2 percent, the church will never be able to challenge things as they are. And, fundamentally, things as they are is the problem. The world is caught in an accelerating spiral of violence—to borrow Dom Helder Camara's image again—which is even now destroying life on earth. If the spiral accelerates to a nuclear level the destruction may become total. But we are not now in a climate of peace, seeking to prevent war. We are in a climate of repressive violence, seeking ways to open our societies to those who have a claim, in justice, on the goods, services, and decision-making processes of the societies of the world. This will involve an opening of conflict in participation—a willingness to give up supremacy for a sense of shared humanity.

The church cannot do this for the human community. But as those who are radically engaged in the world as the scene of God's plan for interhuman justice, the church can seek authentically to be what it has claimed it is, the Body of Christ informed by the Spirit of Justice.

The radical ecumenism of the women's movement in the churches is one possible model for the public, political church; the peace movement may represent still another. That we Christians are not yet totally free of racial, class, and sexual bias does not nullify these efforts—the conflict at the heart of our historical reality must be claimed and dealt with by the church as church. To struggle with our calling to incarnate the Body in justice is our task at this point in history.

Chapter 6 A POSTSCRIPT ON HIERARCHY, POWER, AND AUTHORITY

OF ALL the possible metaphors for the church, the two that need to be heard today in the North American Protestant Church are the Poor and the Body of Christ. The latter is a familiar image, the former is unfamiliar as a designation for the church. Together their strength is a new image that is also rooted in the history of the church.

Much wrangling over the nature of the Protestant Church today centers on the question of authority: who should have it, who does not have it, and how it should be exercised. The nature of the authority of a public, political, and interdenominational church is not obvious. Some would say it is nonexistent. Thus, the nature of authority and its presence (or absence) in the church must be a concern.

Further, it is entirely symptomatic of the contemporary situation that authority needs to be defined carefully. Modernity is characterized by both an erosion of authority and by a lack of clarity about the meaning of authority. Another characteristic of modernity is the ability to turn everything into something else by redefining it. But when this is done with authority, it is defined out of existence.

We need to begin from the beginning and deal with authority in its most traditional sense as that which people obey without losing their freedom.[1] Authority needs to be further distinguished from power, which is the capacity to enforce obedience. Authority is not the same as power. When power must be exercised to enforce obedience, it is a sign of a loss of authority.

A central question needs to be entertained here. Does authority always imply hierarchy? This is the most difficult question, on which the arguments presented in the preceeding five chapters either stand or fall.

The conservative view is that authority is always exercised through coercion and therefore that an authoritarian order must be hierarchical. The liberal view has been that authority is vested in an order of persuasion by reason and therefore must be egalitarian. But, on the one hand, the use of coercion to enforce obedience means that the ruling order has lost authority and cannot expect free obedience, needing to demand it by force. This is most obviously the case in totalitarian regimes in which the rulers must substitute terror for authority.

Yet, on the other hand, argumentation or persuasion equally evidences an erosion of authority. Authority does not explain itself—it must be immediately recognized as authoritative to exist at all.

One of the most enduring sources of authority is neither force nor argumentation, but tradition, a connection to the past, to what has gone before us. What has been believed "everywhere, always and by all" ("ubique, semper, ab omnibus")[2] has the unquestioned force that is authority. The church has exercised authority in this manner. So did the Romans, on whom the church modeled itself. The authority of the traditional has been most often administered through hierarchical orders. The first definition of hierarchical is ecclesiastical.

The trend of the last four centuries has been to question and consequently to undermine the authority of tradition. But the loss of tradition does not mean the loss of the past. In some instances, the loss of tradition has been the welcome destruction of bonds holding each succeeding generation to a predetermined pattern. The danger comes not necessarily from a loss of tradition, but from a loss of the past. Augustine was correct when he claimed that the seat of the mind is in memory. To be conscious of the past is not necessarily to be determined by it. The past contains a vast accumulation that has been only selectively mined. We must search for a usable past that can excite our imaginations and lend our institutions the force of authority. Such rootage in a usable past that is repeatedly reexamined invites participation and is not necessarily hierarchical.

THE BODY OF CHRIST

THIS is the force of the metaphor of the Body of Christ when used in this manner. The Body of Christ as a metaphor connects Christians to the historical events of the life, death, and resurrection of Jesus whom we call the Christ.

But the Body metaphor is also reworked in our contemporary situation. We have noted that the body has been considered in a negative light as the Aristotelian material principle. The Body is deemed to need a "head" or directing spiritual principle. When the metaphor of the Body was applied to women, it conveyed that they were sinful, "fleshly," and subordinate. When the metaphor of the Body was applied to the church, it conveyed that the church too was subordinate and consequently incapable of agency in history.

The Body metaphor needs to be invested with the positive valuation we have come to have of the bodily and the material, and the whole needs to be removed from a mind/body dualism. The Body can thus be seen to evoke the relational connectedness and organic wholeness that do not preclude independence and agency.

This Body contains within itself the capacity for agency, that capacity formerly reserved for Headship. As we no longer separate the body and the mind into opposing concepts, so we need no longer view the Body of Christ as incomplete and lacking direction without a "head."

The very being of the church as the Body of Christ comes about because of the relation of the members to one another. Human connectedness brings God into the world. The Body metaphor coupled with a relational Christology is vested with the authority of its connectedness to the historical Jesus and to the central tenet of the Christian faith, that God was in Christ, while at the same time freeing these traditional concepts from philosophical notions of matter and form, which limited the notion of authority to spiritual heads and material followers.

The relation of the metaphor of the Body of Christ to the historical person Jesus of Nazareth is also important for the connection to the type of person he became. The metaphor of the Body of Christ could be seen to exclude women because of the insistence in some quarters on the maleness of Christ as a criterion for the maleness of the priest. But the maleness of Jesus of Nazareth is fundamentally connected to the type of male he became. Jesus' being in the world was a judgment on patriarchy. His identification with the poor and the oppressed, women prominently among them, is a reversal of traditional roles and a sign of the presence of God. In God, societal roles are broken down (Galatians 3:28) and the human being is graced.

Thus Lord is an inadequate term to apply to either God or Christ, as it denies this central characteristic of Jesus' way of being in the world, which was a criticism of hierarchicalism in all its forms. Jesus himself cautioned the disciples:

> You know that the rulers of the Gentiles lord it over them, and their great men exercise authority over them. It shall not be so among you; but whoever would be great among you must be your servant, and whoever would be first among you must be your slave; even as the [Human One] came not to be served but to serve, and to give his life as a ransom for many.
>
> —Matthew 20: 25-28

The term Lord was introduced as a term for both Jesus and God when the ruling order was itself religious. It may be that the designation of Jesus Christ as Lord was a religious and political necessity in a time when it was crucial to point out that Caesar was not lord. But the consequence was to invest the concept of Christ with the political monarchianism that Jesus himself denounced. The authority Jesus exercised

(Mark 1:22) was not modeled on tyranny but on the service of love.

Authority as shared in service is an image for human relationship to God. Theology has traditionally conceived the relationship of God to humanity as a one-directional exercise of God's authority over humanity. What Jesus revealed about God is that it is God's self-chosen risk to participate with human beings in history, rather than to "Lord" it over them. Human beings, however, have found this understanding of God's authority hard to live with and have frequently projected class notions of domination onto the Godhead. God and the ruling class are deemed to share certain characteristics, and this identification becomes a source of earthly authority to rule.

Jesus himself sought the authority for his teachings in the Jewish traditions, but sought to reclaim and revise them from the perspective of his own interpretation of the contemporary Jewish situation (Mark 2:23-28). Jesus' own style of authority was participation and reciprocity, a sense that authority is rooted in the continuation of the shared community of service.

THE POOR

WHILE the metaphor of the Body of Christ conveys the sense of this shared community over time with which the church has identified itself, the metaphor of the Poor strikes a discordant note. But, I would argue, it is a similarly discordant note to the one Jesus of Nazareth sounded in reworking the traditions he had received. Those who are out of the power structures of the world were the special concern of Jesus of Nazareth. They represent the underside of human history. Through his identification with the poor, Jesus placed them within the history of the church, and their inclusion thus becomes authoritative for Christians.

It is particularly illustrative that those who have been out of power in the world—women, black people, Native Americans, the poor in the so-called third world—have all spent enormous time and energy investigating and publicizing the history of their groups. Women's history, black history, Native American history, and the histories of third-world people, which have proliferated in such quantities in recent decades, are a testimony to the fact that these groups know the authority of their movements is also vested in history.

Reclaiming women's history, for example, has functioned as a way of making visible, of making into public history all the struggles and activities of women that had previously been deemed unimportant and insignificant. Thus the women's movement gains authority for its activities, because it can be shown not only that oppression is an enduring historical phenomenon, but also that women's resistance to these oppressions has always existed. Furthermore, those qualities traditionally associated with the feminine and consequently devalued by the larger society are given status by the fact that so many for so long have acted out of a sense of the importance of these feminine values.

It is significant that the peace movement in recent months has also been turning to the history of resistance to war and the historic arguments against war for a sense of the authority of the peace movement today. The second draft of the Roman Catholic bishops' letter on nuclear arms demonstrates this rootage by the use of the ancient framework of the just war to articulate moral dilemmas in deterrence strategy. But this turning to history is shaped by an appreciation of the crises of contemporary history that make a claim for the concern of Christians. This claim is given a hearing because of the presence in our midst of the Holy Spirit, the justice advocate, who presses us to acknowledge the solidarity of the people of God with the poor.

AUTHORITY AND HIERARCHY

THE authority of a public, political, and interdenominational church lies in the connectedness of this church to the significant events of Christian history, as these are revised and reworked in a contemporary context. The connection of Christians to the historical person of Jesus of Nazareth through the Body of Christ metaphor means that his style of authority becomes authoritative for us in the church today. But this approach to authority needs to be constantly reformed in reference to the significant issues of the contemporary context, a process dynamized by the presence of the Holy Spirit.

One of the key issues in this reformulation is the relationship of authority and hierarchy. Here again an illustration from the women's movement may be useful. Several years ago a significant article by Jo Freeman entitled "The Tyranny of Structurelessness" pointed out that women had discovered that while unstructured interaction might work for consciousness-raising groups, it did not provide a means for the accomplishment of tasks, such as starting a crisis center. Immobilization, hidden and nonaccountable leadership, or elitism were often the result. Groups would bog down in the "pit of process" or leaders would emerge whose personal charisma singled them out, but who were not representative of the group as a whole.[3]

The more recent years of the women's movement have been characterized by a search for structures that facilitate action, but that are open and accountable. It has become evident that the choice in groups is not exclusively between authoritarian or nonauthoritarian structure, but between authority exercised autocratically (whether overtly or covertly) and authority exercised responsibly and in clear and open structures of accountability.

Thus the authority of the public, political, and interdenominational church, which understands itself to be rooted in Christian history but is always undergoing the challenge of the Spirit, can be exercised in accountable and participatory structures that are clear and identifiable. Authority need not go hand in hand with hierarchy, but it does require ordering for its exercise.

Thus inclusivity need not erode authority or preclude its exercise. Structures for the church that facilitate the participation of those who have traditionally been excluded open possibilities of bonding in hitherto unforeseen ways, while not turning away from the inevitable conflicts that such participation will involve. The authority of the church does not rest on the unchallenged exercise of power in its hierarchy, but is based on the church's sense of itself as a continuation of the acts of God in history. Constant reformulation does not erode this sense of self, because from its earliest sources the church has understood itself to be in constant intercourse with the ever-renewing, ever-surprising presence of God in the Holy Spirit: "For by one Spirit we were all baptized into one body [1 Corinthians 12:13]."

Notes

Method

1. Alice Hageman, ed., *Sexist Religion and Women in the Church* (New York: Association Press, 1974), p. 12.

2. Jean Baker Miller, *Toward a New Psychology of Women* (Boston: Beacon Press, 1976), pp. 41 ff.

3. Ibid., p. 41.

4. Paul Minear, *Images of the Church in the New Testament* (Philadelphia: Westminster Press, 1960), p. 23.

5. See Andrew Ortony, ed., *Metaphor and Thought* (Cambridge, England: Cambridge University Press, 1979). This volume is a collection of papers from a conference on metaphor at the University of Illinois at Urbana-Champaign in 1977. The conference addressed the questions "What are metaphors?" and "What are metaphors for?" Each essay gives a different answer. It is, therefore, appropriate to exercise care in using the term metaphor. Max Black warns that there can be no standard rule for determining what is and

what is not a metaphor, and no standard function for metaphor, "because a metaphorical statement involves a rule violation: There can be no rules for 'creatively' violating rules" (Max Black, "More About Metaphor," in Ortony, *Metaphor and Thought*, p. 25).

6. Frederick Herzog, *Justice Church* (Maryknoll, NY: Orbis, 1980), pp. 4-5.

7. Max Black, *Models and Metaphors: Studies in Language and Philosophy* (New York: Cornell University Press, 1972), p. 227.

8. Minear, *Images*, p. 24.

9. Paul Ricoeur, *Hermeneutics and the Human Sciences* (Cambridge: Cambridge University Press, 1981), p. 181.

10. The relationship between doctrine and history is complex and beyond the scope of this study. For the purposes of method, in this work the relationship between doctrine and history is conceived as interactive, that is, ideas are both shaped by and shape history. Since these interactions are intricate, change does not occur synchronomously. The most important concern is an awareness of the dependence of theological viewpoints on social conditions, and a simultaneous concern for the heuristic power of thought in its capacity to transcend social conditions and bring about change through a rise in critical consciousness.

Chapter 1 Women and Metaphor in the History of the Church

1. Edward Schweizer, *Church Order in the New Testament* (London: SCM Press, 1961), pp. 24-25.

2. Minear, *Images*, pp. 111-13.

3. "Declaration on the Question of the Admission of Women to the Priesthood," in Leonard Swidler and Arlene Swidler, eds., *Women Priests: Catholic Commentary on the Vatican Declaration* (New York: Paulist Press, 1977).

4. Elisabeth Schüssler Fiorenza, "The Twelve," in Swidler and Swidler, *Women Priests*, p. 117.

5. Elisabeth Schüssler Fiorenza, "The Apostleship of

Women in Early Christianity," in Swidler and Swidler, *Women Priests*, p. 138.

6. Robin Scroggs, "The Earliest Christian Communities as Sectarian Movement," in J. Neusner, ed., *Christianity, Judaism and Other Greco-Roman Cults*, vol. 2 (Leiden: Brill, 1975), p. 18.

7. Elisabeth Schüssler Fiorenza, "You Are Not to Be Called Father," *Cross Currents* (Fall 1979), p. 305. See also "Women in the Pre-Pauline and Pauline Churches," *Union Seminary Quarterly Review* (Spring and Summer 1979), pp. 153-66; "Biblical Roots for a Discipleship of Equals," *Journal of Pastoral Counseling* (Spring and Summer 1979), pp. 7-15; *In Memory of Her: A Feminist Reconstruction of Christian Origins* (New York: Crossroad, 1983). See also Elisabeth Moltmann-Wendel, *Humanity in God*, Part I (New York: The Pilgrim Press, 1983).

8. Robin Scroggs, "Paul and the Eschatological Women," *Journal of the American Academy of Religion* (1972), p. 291.

9. In the nineteenth-century American women's movement in the church this declaration in Acts became a central tenet of women's claim to exercise their gifts for ministry. See Nancy Hardesty, "Women in the Holiness Movement" and "Feminism in the Evangelical Tradition," in Rosemary Ruether and Eleanor McLaughlin, eds., *Women of Spirit: Female Leadership in the Jewish and Christian Traditions* (New York: Simon & Schuster, 1979), pp. 226-54.

10. Elaine Pagels, *The Gnostic Gospels* (New York: Random House, 1979), p. 63.

11. Ibid., p. 59.

12. Ibid., p. 60.

13. Crouch in I. Balek, "Let Wives Be Submissive . . ." in *The Origin and Apologetic Function of the Household Duty Code (Haustafel) in I Peter* (Ann Arbor, MI: University Microfilms, 1974), p. 9.

14. Wayne Meeks, "The Image of the Androgyne: Uses of a Symbol in Earliest Christianity," *History of Religions* (February 1974), pp. 165-208.

15. Balek, "Let Wives," p. 9.

16. Yves Congar, *L'ecclesiologie du haut moyen age* (Paris: Les Editions du Cerf, 1968), p. 98.

17. Ibid., p. 99.

18. *City of God*, XIV, 28. Trans. Dods.

19. "On Psalm 98," 4, trans. Nicene.

20. Robert Austin Markus, *Saeculum: History and Society in the Theology of St. Augustine* (Cambridge: Cambridge University Press, 1970), pp. 59–71.

21. *City of God*, XIX, 17.

22. Ibid.

23. *Concerning the Nature of Good*, III.

24. *Homilies on I Timothy*, 9, 1 (PG, 62, 543 C-545 B).

25. *On the Priesthood*, 2, 2 (PG 48, 633 AB) trans. Nicene and Post-Nicene Fathers, 1st series IX, p. 49.

26. Jeffrey Burton Russell, *A History of Medieval Christianity: Prophecy and Order* (New York: Thomas Y. Crowell, 1968), p. 40.

27. Minear, *Images*, p. 63.

28. Rosemary Ruether, "Liberation Mariology," *The Other Side* (May 1979), p. 18.

29. Ernest W. McDonnell, *The Beguines and Beghards in Medieval Culture* (Dallas: Taylor Publishing Co., 1954), p. 141.

30. Herbert Grundmann, *Religiöse Bewegungen in Mittelalter*, 2d rev. ed. (Darmstadt, 1961), chaps. 4, 5, and 6.

31. The scholarship that does exist on the Beguine movement is limited and found largely in scattered articles. Most studies appear in German and French. The bibliography found in McDonnell, *Beguines and Beghards*, is exhaustive for the period up to the early 1960s. Two major articles of the 1970s are: "Comment on fait des hérétiques," review article in J.C. Schmitt, *Mort d'une hérésie* (Paris, 1978), pp. 189-93; R.E. Lerner, "Image of Mixed Liquids in Late Medieval Thought," *Church History* (December 1971), pp. 397-411.

32. McDonnell, *Beguines and Beghards*, chap. 1.

33. Hilka Alfans, "Altfranzösische Mystik und Beginentum," *Zeitschrift für romanische Philologie* 47 (1927): 160.

34. McDonnell, *Beguines and Beghards,* p. 143.

35. Ibid., p. 123.

36. Other understandings are also in evidence among the leadership of the medieval church. In many ways Cistercian and Franciscan spirituality, emphasizing poverty, was very influential in the period 1300 to 1600 and led to conflicts that contributed to the Protestant Reformation. This sketch must therefore not be taken as exhaustive, nor indicative of any single self-understanding in the medieval church.

37. Ernst Troeltsch, *The Social Teachings of the Christian Churches* (New York: Macmillan, 1949), vols. 1 and 2, but especially vol. 1, pp. 328-82.

38. This use of the categories of Troeltsch to describe the modern American denomination is suggested by the work of Langdon Gilkey, *How the Church Can Minister to the World Without Losing Itself* (New York: Harper & Row, 1964), p. 7.

39. Sydney Mead, "From Denominationalism to Americanism," *Journal of Religion* (January 1956), pp. 2-6; Mead quotes Henry F. May, *Protestant Churches and Industrial America* (New York: Harper & Row, 1949), p. 91.

40. Martin Marty, *Religious Empire* (New York: Dial Press, 1970), p. 69.

41. Ann Douglas, *The Feminization of American Culture* (New York: Knopf, 1977), pp. 50-93. Douglas' thesis obviously does not apply to women of color and poor white women such as the mill workers. But the image of a glorified domesticity was held up to all as the ideal of womanhood.

42. Ibid., p. 131.

43. R. Pierce Beaver, *All Loves Excelling: American Protestant Women in World Mission* (Grand Rapids, MI: Eerdmans, 1968), p. 52.

44. Winifred Matthews, *Dauntless Women* (New York: Friendship Press, 1947), p. 12.

45. Alice L. Hageman, "Women and Missions: The Cost of Liberation," in Alice L. Hageman, *Sexist Religion,* p. 173.

46. Quoted in Beaver, *All Loves,* pp. 112-13.

47. Hageman, "Women and Missions," pp. 178-79.

48. Sydney Ahlstrom, *A Religious History of the American People* (New Haven: Yale University Press, 1972), p. 472.

49. Edward Deming Andrews, *The People Called Shakers* (New York: Dover, 1963), pp. 97-99.

50. Nordi Reeck Campion, *Ann the Word: The Life of Mother Ann Lee, Founder of the Shakers* (Boston: Little, Brown & Co., 1976), p. 87.

51. While celibacy may not appear "liberating" to modern eyes, the freedom from constant childbearing and its health hazards was a step for women away from constant identification with the body.

52. Mary Baker Eddy, *Introspection and Retrospection* (Boston: A.V. Stewart, 1892), p. 76.

53. H. Shelton Smith, Robert Handy, and Lefferts Loetscher, *American Christianity*, vol. 2 (New York: Charles Scribner's Sons, 1960-63), p. 229.

54. Barbara Brown Zikmund, "The Feminist Thrust of Sectarian Christianity," in Ruether and McLaughlin, *Women of Spirit*, p. 220.

55. Mary Baker Eddy, *Science and Health: With Key to the Scriptures* (Boston: A.V. Stewart, 1910), p. 517.

Chapter 2   Metaphors for the Contemporary Church

1. Yves Congar, *Christians actives* (Paris: Editions du Cerf, 1962), p. 71. (Italics added to exclusive language.)

2. Gustavo Gutiérrez, *A Theology of Liberation* (Maryknoll, NY: Orbis, 1973), pp. 57-65.

3. Ibid., p. 65.

4. Ibid.

5. Leonardo Boff, *Jesus Christ Liberator* (Maryknoll, NY: Orbis, 1978), p. 280.

6. Gutiérrez, *A Theology*, p. 237.

7. José Míguez Bonino, *Doing Theology in a Revolutionary Situation* (Philadelphia: Fortress Press, 1975), pp. 22-23.

8. Ibid., pp. 154-73.

9. Quoted in Joyce Hollyday, "Leaven of the People," *Sojourners* (December 1980), p. 24.

10. Ibid., p. 24.

11. Quoted from a speech at the funeral in Hollyday, "Leaven," p. 24.

12. Rosemary Radford Ruether, "Basic Communities: Renewal at the Roots," *Christianity and Crisis*, September 21, 1981, p. 234.

13. Hollyday, "Leaven," p. 23.

14. Ed Grace, "Italy: Disobedience as Witness," *Christianity and Crisis*, September 21, 1981, p. 245.

15. Cora Ferro, "The Latin American Woman: The Praxis and Theology of Liberation," in Sergio Torres and John Eagleson, eds., *The Challenge of Basic Christian Communities* (Maryknoll, NY: Orbis, 1981), pp. 33, 36.

16. Phillip Berryman, "Latin America: 'Iglesia que Nace del Pueblo,'" *Christianity and Crisis*, September 21, 1981, p. 241.

17. See Torres and Eagleson, *Challenge*, published in North America in 1981 by Orbis to facilitate discussion of this movement.

18. Robert Bellah. *The Broken Covenant* (New York: Crossroad/Seabury, 1975), chap. 2, "America as Chosen People," pp. 36-60.

19. See Sidney Mead, "The Nation with the Soul of a Church," in *American Civil Religion*, Russell R. Richey and Donald G. Jones, eds. (New York: Harper & Row, 1974), p. 60.

20. See Ahlstrom, *Religious History*, p. 82.

21. Frederick Herzog, *Liberation Theology* (New York: Seabury, 1972), p. viii.

22. Hugo Assmann, *Theology for a Nomad Church* (Maryknoll, NY: Orbis, 1976), p. 16.

23. Frederick Herzog, "Introduction: On Liberating Liberation Theology," in Assmann, *Nomad Church*, p. 10.

24. Robert Jewett, *The Captain America Complex* (Philadelphia: Westminster Press, 1973), p. 33.

25. See Gayraud Wilmore and James H. Cone, *Black The-*

ology: A Documentary History 1966-1979 (Maryknoll, NY: Orbis, 1979), especially part 2.

26. Herzog, *Justice Church*, p. 96.

27. Ibid., chap. 3, pp. 55-71.

Chapter 3   A Christ for the Body

1. Rosemary Ruether, *Faith and Fratricide* (New York: Seabury, 1974); *To Change the World: Christology and Cultural Criticism* (New York: Crossroad, 1981), pp. 31-43.

2. Alan Davies, *Anti-Semitism and the Foundations of Christianity* (Paramus, NJ: Paulist/Newman Press, 1979), pp. 188-207, 246-50.

3. Gabriel Fackre, *The Christian Story* (Grand Rapids, MI: Eerdmans, 1978), p. 23.

4. Unpublished lecture to the Association of Professors and Researchers in Religious Education, 1981.

5. *Theological Dictionary of the New Testament* (Grand Rapids, MI: Eerdmans, 1967), pp. 1099 ff.

6. Aristotle, *On the Generation of Animals*, 1, 20, 23.

7. Thomas Aquinas, *Summa Theologica*, part 1, question 92, article 2. (Italics in original.)

8. Ibid., part 3, supplement, question 39.

9. John Saward, *Christ and His Bride* (London: Church Literature Association, 1977), p. 5.

10. *Vatican Declaration, Commentary*, p. 20.

11. Saward, *Christ*, p. 10.

12. Peter Damian, Sermon 18 (P. L. 144: 607).

13. St. Anselm, "Epistola de sacramentis ecclesiae," in Franciscus S. Schmitt, *Opera Omnia* (Edinburgh: Thomas Nelson & Son, 1970), vol. 2, p. 240.

14. Anselm, *Meditation*, 17, Schmitt, vol. 3, pp. 86-87.

15. Bernard of Clairveaux, Grat. 13.43 (Leclercq-Rochais 3.196).

16. Saward, *Christ*, p. 10.

17. Eric Neumann, *Depth Psychology and a New Ethic*, trans. Rolfe (London: Hodder & Stoughton, 1969), p. 53.

18. Miller, *New Psychology*, p. 57.

19. Mary Daly, *Beyond God the Father* (Boston: Beacon Press, 1974), p. 77.

20. Dell Martin, *Battered Wives* (New York: Pocket Books, Inc., 1976), p. 2.

21. Gottschalk (Godescalc d'Orbais), "De Praedestinatione," in D.C. Lambot, *Oeuvres Théologiques et Grammaticales de Godescalc D'Orbais* (Lovrain: Spicilegium Sacrum Lovaniese, 1945), p. 204.

22. Augustine, *Iojannis Evangelium*, 110.2.

23. Friedrich Schleiermacher, *The Christian Faith*, H.R. Macintosh and J.S. Stewart, eds. (Edinburgh: T. & T. Clark, 1928), pp. 374 ff.

24. Joseph Bellamy, *True Religion Delineated or Experimental Religion* (Boston: S. Kneeland, 1850), pp. 269-70.

25. See H.S. Smith, ed., *Horace Bushnell* (New York: Oxford University Press, 1965). Bushnell's view of the atonement is far more complex than I am allowing here. In his later work, *Forgiveness and Law*, he corrects the overly liberal ideas of his earlier work. Yet it is the former line of thought that his successors follow.

26. Smith, *Bushnell*, pp. 280-82.

27. Douglas, *Feminization*, pp. 146-47.

28. Horace Bushnell, *Women's Suffrage: Reform Against Nature* (New York: Charles Scribner, 1869), p. 66.

29. *Testimonies of the Life, Character of Revelations and Doctrines of Mother Ann Lee* (Albany, NY: Weed, Parsons & Co., 1888), p. 268.

30. Andrew Jackson Davis, "Ann Lee," in Gibes B. Avery, ed., *Sketches of Shakers and Shakerism* (Albany, NY: Weed, Carsons & Co., 1884), p. 29.

31. Eddy, *Science and Health*, p. 517.

32. Gutiérrez, *A Theology*, p. 173.

33. Boff, *Jesus Christ Liberator*, pp. 204-5.

34. Ibid., p. 279.

35. Ibid., p. 274.

36. Herzog, *Justice Church*, p. 61.

37. Ruether, *Christology*, pp. 54-55.

38. Gutiérrez, *A Theology*, p. 161.
39. Ibid., p. 161.
40. Ibid., p. 163.
41. Boff, *Jesus Christ Liberator*, p. 207.
42. Ibid., p. 207.
43. Ruether, *Christology*, p. 42.
44. Ibid., p. 42.
45. Tom Driver, *Christ in a Changing World* (New York: Crossroad, 1981), p. 15.
46. Robert Terry, "White Male Club: Biology and Power," in *Racism/Sexism, Where Are We?* St. Cloud University, St. Cloud, MN, Video/recording copy, 1977, Louis Costanzo, producer, p. 3/5.
47. Gloria Joseph and Jill Lewis, *Common Differences: Conflicts in Black and White Feminist Perspectives* (New York: Doubleday, 1981), especially part 2, pp. 43-71.
48. Carter Heyward, *The Redemption of God* (Washington, DC: University Press of America, 1982), p. 12.
49. Driver, *Christ*, p. 16.
50. Heyward, *Redemption*, p. 15.
51. Driver, *Christ*, pp. 23-26.
52. Heyward, *Redemption*, p. xv. Used by permission.
53. Driver, *Christ*, p. 40.
54. Ibid., p. 44.
55. Ibid., p. 51.
56. *Boston Globe*, May 22, 1982, p. A1.
57. Heyward, *Redemption*, p. 159.

Chapter 4   The Spirit of Justice

1. Paul Tillich, *Systematic Theology*, vol. 3 (Chicago: University of Chicago Press, 1963), pp. 293-94. See also André Manaranche, *L'Esprit et la Femme* (Paris: Editions du Seuil, 1973), especially pp. 61-77.
2. Schleiermacher, *The Christian Faith*, pp. 374, 395, 399.
3. Jürgen Moltmann, *The Trinity and the Kingdom* (New York: Harper & Row, 1981), p. 136.

4. Ibid., p. 131.

5. In the Western context, the function of the phrase was to interpret the creed for the pastoral purpose of again securing the divinity of Christ. The result, however, was a controversy with the Eastern Church, which produced schism in 1054. The schism was due as well to issues like the right of the pope to fix and revise the norm of Orthodoxy, especially a source of tension with the Eastern Church's norm of antiquity as a rule of faith, and over the dominance of Augustinian thought in the West. But the double procession of the Spirit played a major role in bringing about the separation into two churches.

6. Hans Küng and Jürgen Moltmann, eds., *Conflicts About the Holy Spirit* (New York: Seabury Press, 1979), part 1, pp. 3-30.

7. Tillich, *Systematic Theology*, p. 149.

8. Ibid., p. 149.

9. John Calvin, *Institutes of the Christian Religion* (Philadelphia: Westminster Press, 1960), pp. 47, 79).

10. Bernard Holm, "The Work of the Spirit: The Reformation to the Present," in Paul D. Opsahl, ed., *The Holy Spirit in the Life of the Church* (Minneapolis: Augsburg, 1978), p. 108.

11. Paul Tillich, *Perspectives on 19th and 20th Century Protestant Theology*, Carl E. Braaten, ed. (New York: Harper & Row, 1967), pp. 9, 24-90.

12. José Míguez Bonino, "Welsey's Doctrine of Sanctification from a Liberationist Perspective," in Theodore Runyon, ed., *Sanctification and Liberation* (Nashville, TN: Abingdon Press, 1981), pp. 53-55.

13. Schleiermacher, *The Christian Faith*, pp. 377, 562.

14. Karl Barth, *Dogmatics in Outline* (New York: Harper & Row, 1959), p. 126.

15. Ibid., p. 132.

16. Karl Barth, *Church Dogmatics I* (Edinburgh: T. & T. Clark, 1975), p. 359.

17. See ibid., p. 332.

18. Robert S. Ellwood, in Richard Quebedeaux, *The*

Worldly Evangelicals (New York: Harper & Row, 1978), p. 166.

19. Dean William Ferm, "Protestant Liberalism Reaffirmed," *The Christian Century*, April 28, 1976, p. 411.

20. Susan Thistlethwaite, review of Dean William Ferm, *Contemporary American Theologies: A Critical Survey* in *Religious Education* (September-October 1982), p. 579.

21. Schleiermacher, *Christian Faith*, pp. 469-73.

22. Ibid., p. 562.

23. Ibid., p. 450.

24. Dean William Ferm, *Contemporary American Theologies, A Critical Survey* (New York: Seabury Press, 1981), pp. 45-48, 83.

25. Schleiermacher, *Christian Faith*, p. 531.

26. Miller, *New Psychology*, p. 65.

27. Douglas, *Feminization*, chap. 4, "The Loss of Theology," pp. 143–96.

28. Carol Gilligan, *In a Different Voice: Psychological Theory and Women's Development* (Cambridge: Harvard University Press, 1982).

29. Herzog, *Justice Church*, p. 40.

30. Tillich, *Systematic Theology*, p. 148.

31. Moltmann, *Trinity and the Kingdom*, p. 58.

32. Herzog, *Liberation Theology*, p. 189. (Italics added to exclusive language.)

33. Ibid., p. 190.

34. Julius Lester, quoted in Herzog, *Liberation Theology*, pp. 190-91.

35. Leonardo Boff, *Way of the Cross, Way of Justice* (Maryknoll, NY: Orbis, 1980), p. 5. Used by permission.

36. William Marson, *The Gospel of Luke* (New York: Harper & Row, n.d.), pp. 41-42. (Italics added.)

37. Paulo Freire, *Pedagogy of the Oppressed* (New York: Herder & Herder, 1970), p. 55.

38. Dorothee Soelle, "Thou Shalt Have No Other Jeans Before Me," in *The Challenge of Liberation Theology: A First World Response*, Brian Mahan and L. Dale Richesin, eds. (Maryknoll, NY: Orbis, 1981), pp. 4-16.

39. Dorothee Soelle, "Resistance: Toward a First World Theology," *Christianity and Crisis*, July 23, 1979, p. 188.

40. Ibid., p. 180.

41. Ibid., p. 179; see also Leon Howell, "C.C.N.V.: Resistance in Flower in the First World's Capital," *Christianity and Crisis*, July 23, 1979, pp. 182–87.

42. Freire, *Pedagogy of the Oppressed*, p. 26.

43. John Rawls, *A Theory of Justice* (Oxford: Oxford University Press, 1972).

Chapter 5 Locations

1. Statistics from Judith L. Weidman, ed., *Women Ministers: How Women Are Redefining Traditional Roles* (San Francisco: Harper & Row, 1981), pp. 2-11.

2. Edward C. Lehmann Jr. and the Task Force on Women in Ministry of the Ministers Council of the American Baptist Churches; *Project S.W.I.M.: A Study of Women in Ministry* (n.d., mimeographed). Quoted in Barbara Wheeler, "Accountability to Women in Theological Seminaries," *Religious Education* (July-August 1981), p. 384.

3. Mary Elizabeth Hunt, "Women Ministering in Mutuality: The Real Connections," *Sisters Today* (August-September 1979), p. 40, quoting Carole Etzler, *Sometimes I Wish*, Sisters Unlimited, Atlanta, GA.

4. Hunt, "Women Ministering," p. 41.

5. Ibid., p. 40.

6. Ibid., p. 37, quoting a *New York Times* article, October 8, 1979.

7. Ibid., quoting a *New York Times* article, October 26, 1979.

8. Hunt, "Women Ministering," p. 38.

9. See "Women in Clergy Would Support Gay Ordination," *Keeping You Posted* (February 1979), and letter of Martha B. Kriebel, et al., to UCC clergywomen, May 1979.

10. Mary Elizabeth Hunt, "Roman Catholic Ministry, Patriarchal Past, Feminist Future," in *New Woman, New Church, New Priestly Ministry: Proceedings of the Second*

Conference on the Ordination of Roman Catholic Women, November 10-12, 1978, Baltimore, MD. (Rochester, NY: Kirkwood Press, 1980), p. 33.

11. Constance F. Parvey, ed., *Ordination of Women in Ecumenical Perspective*, Faith and Order Paper 105 (Geneva: World Council of Churches, 1980), p. 33.

12. Letty Russell, *Women and Unity: Problem or Possibility?* Report to the Commission on Faith and Order, National Council of the Churches of Christ, Stoney Point, NY, March 27, 1981, p. 1.

13. Ibid., p. 1.

14. Ibid., p. 2.

15. "Authority-in-Community," drafted by Madeline Boucher for the Commission on Faith and Order, National Council of the Churches of Christ, Stoney Point, NY, March 27-29, 1981.

16. The Cornwall Collective, *Your Daughters Shall Prophesy: Feminist Alternatives in Theological Education* (New York: The Pilgrim Press, 1980).

17. Boucher, "Authority-in-Community," p. 3 (italics in original).

18. Ibid., p. 20.

19. Ibid., p. 21 (italics in original).

20. See Frances Beale, "Double Jeopardy: To Be Black and Female," in Wilmore and Cone, *Black Theology*, pp. 374-75.

21. "Women's Theological Center: A Prospectus," n.d., Women's Theological Center publication, 400 The Fenway, Boston, MA.

22. Thomas Hoyt, "Liberation and the Task of Systematic Theology," response to Frederick Herzog's *Justice Church*, working paper, American Academy of Religion Annual Meeting, San Francisco, CA, 1981, p. 6.

23. Martin Luther King, *Where Do We Go from Here: Chaos or Community?* (Boston: Beacon Press, 1968), p. 86.

24. *Time*, November 8, 1982, p. 16.

25. *Christianity and Crisis*, May 2, 1983, p. 155.

26. *Time*, May 16, 1983, p. 65.

27. *The Boston Globe*, May 8, 1983, p. A26.

28. Two of the most serious, and related problems are: (1) the conflicting evangelical and rationalistic arguments employed in the letter and (2) the connection of the moral arguments against nuclear weapons and the antiabortion stance of the Roman Catholic Church. While appealing to evangelically based ethics in the introduction to their letter, the bishops ultimately decide their case on Just War Theory. No sustained attempt is made to adjudicate between these arguments. The antiabortion arguments are linked to the Just War argumentation. Similarly no attempt is made to discuss difficulties in this stance from an evangelical viewpoint. Nevertheless, the political impact of the letter is the point of its mention here.

29. Alan Geyer, *The Idea of Disarmament* (Elgin, IL: Brethren Press, 1982), p. 191.

30. *National Catholic Reporter*, quoted in *Time*, November 8, 1982.

31. Miller, *New Psychology*, pp. 13-20, 127-33.

32. Ruth Leger Sivard, *World Military and Social Expenditures* (Leesburg, VA: World Priorities, 1982), pp. 5-6.

Chapter 6   A Postscript on Hierarchy, Power, and Authority

1. Hannah Arendt, "What Is Authority?" in *Between Past and Future* (New York: Penguin Books, 1980), p. 106.

2. Jaroslav Pelikan, *The Christian Tradition*, vol. 1, *The Emergence of the Catholic Tradition* (Chicago: University of Chicago Press, 1971), p. 333.

3. Cornwall Collective, *Your Daughters*, p. 59.